Community Arts for God's Purposes

Kristin van Lieshout

- Meet
- Specify
- Connect
- Analyze
- Spark
- Improve
- Celebrate

Community Arts for God's Purposes

How to Create Local Artistry Together

Brian Schrag & Julisa Rowe

WILLIAM CAREY PUBLISHING
Available at missionbooks.org

Community Arts for God's Purposes: How to Create Local Artistry Together

Copyright © 2020 by GEN (Global Ethnodoxology Network)

All rights reserved. No part of this book may be reproduced, stored in a retrieval system, or transmitted in any form or by any means—electronic, mechanical, photocopy, recording, or otherwise—without prior written permission of the publisher, except brief quotations used in connection with reviews in magazines or newspapers. For permission, email permissions@wclbooks.com.

All Scripture quotations, unless otherwise indicated, are from the Holy Bible, New International Version® (NIV®), copyright © 1973, 1978, 1984, 2011 by Biblica, Inc.™ Used by permission of Zondervan. All rights reserved worldwide. www.zondervan.com

The "NIV" and "New International Version" are trademarks registered in the United States Patent and Trademark Office by Biblica, Inc.™

Scripture quotations marked NLT are from the Holy Bible, New Living Translation.® copyright © 1996, 2004, 2007 by Tyndale House Foundation. Used by permission of Tyndale House Publishers, Inc., Carol Stream, Illinois 60188. All rights reserved.

Published by William Carey Publishing
10 W. Dry Creek Cir
Littleton, CO 80120 | www.missionbooks.org

William Carey Publishing is a ministry of Frontier Ventures
Pasadena, CA 91104 | www.frontierventures.org

Mike Riester, cover and interior design
Cover art painted by Kristin van Lieshout
Julie Johnson, simplification editor

ISBN: 978-1-64508-180-7 (English paperback)

Printed Worldwide

24 23 22 21 20   1 2 3 4 5   IN

Library of Congress Control Number: 2019918747

CONTENTS

Preface vii
Prepare Yourself xi

USE THE *CREATING LOCAL ARTS TOGETHER* METHOD

Creating Local Arts Together (CLAT) Summary:
Step 1: Meet a Community and Its Artistic Genres 1
Step 2: Specify Kingdom Goals 7
Step 3: Connect Genres to Goals 15
Step 4: Analyze Genres and Events 19
Step 5: Spark Creativity 39
Step 6: Improve Results 47
Step 7: Celebrate and Integrate for Continuity 49

CLOSING

1: Community Arts Profile (CAP) Outline 51
2: Summary Decision Rubric 54
3: Creating Local Arts Together (CLAT) Summary 55

FIGURES

Fig. 01 Careful Contextualization xiv
Fig. 02 Simple Arts Engagement Activities xxvi
Fig. 03 Creating Local Arts Together xxviii
Fig. 04 Creating Local Arts Together (CLAT): A Summary xxxii
Fig. 05 Studying the Community: Some Questions to Ask 2
Fig. 06 How to Recognize Artistic Communication Acts 3
Fig. 07 Sample Mono (DR Congo) Genre Comparison Chart 4
Fig. 08 Simplified Overview of Connecting Genre to Goals 16
Fig. 09 Advice for Audio and Visual Recording 20
Fig. 10 Characteristics of an Artistic Event Suitable for Study 20
Fig. 11 Categories of Performance Features 27
Fig. 12 Things to Write Down When Designing a Sparking Activity 45
Fig. 13 An Approach to Effective Evaluation 48

PREFACE

This manual introduces concepts that are new to many people, such as the "Big Ideas" listed here. The rest of the manual will expand on these ideas.

Big Ideas

Systems of artistic creativity have interlocking components: knowledge, skills, physical resources, social patterns, and people in various roles.

Creative systems are difficult to describe fully. Not many people in any community can adequately describe their own creative systems. The process in this manual helps reveal the dynamics and details of such systems.

No artistic form communicates intended messages universally.

People often say, "Music is a universal language."[1] They believe this statement is true. They believe music communicates the same way in every culture. This saying comes from American poet Henry Wadsworth Longfellow. Longfellow does state that "[m]usic is the universal language of mankind—poetry their universal pastime and delight." However, he is celebrating the musical variety displayed in Italian, Swiss, Scotch, English, and Spanish songs. He does not intend to say music will look the same in every culture. Music and other arts exist universally. However, every kind of artistic communication takes forms and meanings particular to each community.

Local creativity has essential benefits that outside creativity doesn't provide.

The benefits of local creativity include more penetrating, relevant, memorable, and engaging communication for education and motivation.

---

1 Henry Wadsworth Longfellow, *Outre-Mer: A Pilgrimage beyond the Sea* (1833; repr. Boston: Houghton, Mifflin, and Co., 1883), 197.

Every community can benefit from more local creativity.

Every community needs more local creativity. Ethnolinguistic minorities whose arts are stagnant or dying may need local creativity most urgently.

Specific kinds of creativity can help communities reach their goals.

This field manual describes a seven-step method. The method is called Creating Local Arts Together (CLAT; also known as cocreation). In communities that have followed these steps, good things have happened.

An arts advocate who implements the seven-step method can positively affect local creativity.

An arts advocate may be a community insider, outsider, or someone who knows both identities.

An arts advocate's primary job is encouraging others to make new artistic things.

An arts advocate's posture toward a community is one of learning, dialoguing, facilitating, and encouraging.

Learn about a community's artistic genres first.

The foundation for everything in this manual is understanding the arts that a community identifies with and uses. So the community's first task is to make a list of local artistic genres ("Take a First Glance at a Community's Arts," Step 1). In Step 4, you'll find how the Euro-American artistic domains of music, dance, drama, oral/verbal arts, and visual arts relate to local genres. But starting with the community's genres is less confusing than beginning with Western categories. So start with the local classifications.

We best understand the Church's current mission on Earth in relationship to God's bigger story: God created the universe, humans broke their relationship with God, Jesus brought the kingdom of Heaven, and God will make everything right in the new Heavens and the new Earth.

A group of Christians must not only develop the arts that their particular history has produced; rather, they must also be aware of God's artistry. They must be mindful of their artistry's purposes in the rest of God's creation and in Heaven.

Who Should Use the Creating Local Arts Together Approach?

We originally planned the manual as a tool for Christians working professionally in cross-cultural contexts. This could include missionaries, international aid workers, and others. However, the method introduced here applies to many situations that are less cross-cultural. One worship leader in a local church said, "I need to do this. I need to get to know my congregation first. Then I can encourage different kinds of artists to create new things for God's purposes."

Preface

His statement makes sense. Every individual human represents unique experiences, ideas, neurological connections, physical qualities, emotions, and other characteristics that no other person can entirely know. If you want to engage with people of a different language, worldview, geography, diet, and social patterns, you will need to expend much effort and use many skills. We provide rigorous research and other activities to help you.

You could also apply the approach to people who are very much like you—your best friend, or your spouse. In fact, you could follow the CLAT process to learn something new about your own artistic gifts and life goals. You could create something artistic to improve your own future.

We mostly use examples of people crossing large cultural barriers. But don't let that stop you from finding other applications.

History and Acknowledgments

Let's call this book the Abridged CLAT Manual. We created it by drawing the most essential information from two books: *Worship and Mission for the Global Church: An Ethnodoxology Handbook* and *Creating Local Arts Together: A Manual to Help Communities Reach Their Kingdom Goals* (William Carey Library, 2013). Many people contributed their gifts to these two volumes. The Abridged CLAT Manual makes these collections of wisdom available to a larger group, emphasizing the most practical ideas and tools.

This manual is saturated with centuries of ideas and events, but it is geared toward understanding the present. It is directed by a vision of a better future: the kingdom of Heaven. Contributors derived insight from academic disciplines such as ethnomusicology, folklore, performance studies, anthropology, biblical studies, and missiology. Examples of artistic contributions from two thousand years of church history also inspired and guided us. More recently, we owe most of our approach to people who were pioneers in applying ethnomusicology to Christian aims, including Vida Chenoweth, Roberta King, and Tom Avery. Finally, this manual would not have been possible without the energy and connections that Robin Harris and the Global Ethnodoxology Network (GEN) have provided.

The Abridged CLAT Manual is an imperfect object that will continue to grow. It will spawn new objects with different shapes in different places. We take responsibility for its current contour and content. We also are accountable for errors and omissions. Now it's yours. You may take it, play with it, add to it, or discard parts of it. Now you have the responsibility to use this manual. Let it be an aid to helping others create astounding bits of artistry on Earth that you'll recognize in Heaven.

Brian Schrag and Julisa Rowe, 2020

Notes on Versions

Since 2017, this Abridged CLAT Manual has included changes to some of the names of the CLAT process itself. We made these changes after years of teaching the material in Arts for a Better Future classes. The new words make the whole process clearer, and make teaching it easier. Here is a comparison of the original and new vocabulary:

Step	Original (2013)	Revised (2020)
1	**Meet** a Community and Its Arts	**Meet** a Community and Its Artistic Genres
2	**Specify** Kingdom Goals	**Specify** Kingdom Goals
3	**Select** Effects, Content, Genre, & Events	**Connect** Genres to Goals
4	**Analyze** an Event Containing the Chosen Genre(s)	**Analyze** Genres and Events
5	**Spark** Creativity	**Spark** Creativity
6	**Improve** New Works	**Improve** Results
7	**Integrate** and Celebrate for Continuity	**Celebrate** and Integrate for Continuity

PREPARE YOURSELF

All the Arts
From All the World
For All of God's Purposes

REALITY: People communicate in over seven thousand languages around the world. People convey ideas by spoken words. They also communicate artistically through song, drama, dance, visual art, story, and other means.

REALITY: All communities have imperfect relationships with God. All communities struggle with social upheaval, violence, disease, anger, sexual immorality, anxiety, and fear.

REALITY: God gave every community unique gifts of artistic communication to tell the Truth. He gave every community unique gifts of artistic communication to bring healing and hope and joy in response to problems. Many of these gifts, however, lie unused, misused, or dying.

The purpose of this manual is to guide your involvement in working toward a new reality. The new reality is one in which all cultures use all of their gifts to worship, obey, and enjoy God with all of their heart, soul, mind, and strength (Mark 12:30). In other words, this manual will help you work alongside local musicians, dancers, actors, painters, sculptors, storytellers, and other artists. It will help you work together to inspire the creation of new songs, dances, dramas, paintings, sculptures, and stories. It will help you to help people bring God's kingdom into their communities.

We have organized our arts activities according to how they can move us toward the kingdom of God. What is his kingdom? Jesus taught his followers to pray for the kingdom of God to come to Earth (Matt 6:10). He described God's kingdom as centered on himself and his message (Mark 1:15). Jesus said the kingdom of God grows to great size, but no one can explain how it grows (Mark 4). God's kingdom maintains values different from the values of human social systems (Mark 10, 12; Luke 6). Healing and spiritual warfare accompany it (Luke 9, 11). On Earth, God's kingdom tangibly reflects Heaven. God wants us to help expand his kingdom on Earth.

The kingdom of God only partially exists on Earth now. Currently, every community has aspects that are more like the kingdom and aspects that are less like the kingdom. No human culture fully expresses God's kingdom. But because God created the human race in his image, glimpses of his kingdom are everywhere.

What does a community look like when it is deeply shaped by the values and spiritual power of God's kingdom? It contains an expanding body of Christ-followers who worship God in spirit and in truth. Its members grow healthier spiritually, socially, and physically. Older members pass on God-reflecting aspects of their cultures to younger members. Everyone in the community has access to accurate Scripture in the language they understand best. Young and old remember Scripture and apply it to their lives. Justice, honesty, health, and joy mark the whole community. Community members care for and love marginalized people.

 Discuss examples you've seen that demonstrate Heaven on Earth

Locally available artistic forms of communication are powerful resources. Local artistic expression is embedded in culture. It touches many important aspects of a society. It identifies important messages, separating them from everyday activities. Local artistic expression touches people intellectually. It also gives them an emotional experience. Local artistic expression helps people remember what they heard. It increases a message's impact through multiple media that often include the whole body. It concentrates the information contained in a message. It instills solidarity in its performers and experiencers. Local artistic expression provides socially acceptable frameworks for expressing difficult or new ideas. It inspires and moves people to action. It can act as a strong sign of identity. It also opens spaces for people to imagine and dream. Perhaps most importantly, local artistic communication exists, and is owned, locally. Translation of foreign materials is not needed. Rather, local artists are empowered to contribute to the expansion of the kingdom of God.

 Discuss examples you've seen of the special powers of artistic communication.

Our method helps you and a community work together. It helps you decide together which characteristics of the kingdom of God the community wants to cultivate. We show you how to look for local artistic genres to accomplish the community's kingdom goals. We provide activities throughout the manual, giving you ideas for inspiring creativity in the local genres. We show you how to join in others' creativity. We want to join in others' creativity because we want to help people use their existing arts for new purposes, and we want to see these purposes continue into the future.

Our Model: The Three Phases of Jesus's Life

This is how Paul described Jesus's ministry on Earth:

> [I]n humility value others above yourselves, not looking to your own interests but each of you to the interests of the others. In your relationships with one another, have the same mindset as Christ Jesus: Who, being in very nature God, did not consider equality with God something to be used to his own advantage; rather, he made himself nothing by taking the very nature of a servant, being made in human likeness. And being found in appearance as a man, he humbled himself by becoming obedient to death—even death on a cross!
>
> —Philippians 2:3b-8

Three parts of Jesus's incarnation show how we should do mission:

1. **Be with.** Jesus left his "home culture" with God the Father and joined humanity in Palestine (Earth). Our first task in mission is to live with people in community and make relationships.

2. **Learn from.** Jesus learned from human beings in his Palestinian community for almost thirty years before he began his full ministry. Our second interaction as arts facilitators is to ask people about their community's arts and goals. We show them love by learning from them. This process may happen over a long time.

3. **Work toward.** Only after going to humans and learning from them for three decades did Jesus announce and fulfill his purpose publicly (Matt 4:23). He worked side-by-side with his disciples toward the goals of his kingdom.
   Our third missional activity, after going to people and learning from them, is to work toward goals with them. As arts facilitators, we do this by exploring with our friends and colleagues in the community how we might work together to use their arts to meet their goals.

When your work becomes complex, remind yourself of these three basic activities.

All?

The title of this section uses the word "all" three times. What do we mean? "All the arts" doesn't suggest that God wants every art form in its current state in his kingdom. Rather, we want to approach every art graciously. We don't want to judge an art form's worth or usefulness for the kingdom until God judges it. All communities and their arts are flawed by sin, but God can redeem all things. The process of integrating arts into the kingdom requires re-creation. (See Figure 1 for the process of evaluation we use, called "Careful Contextualization.")

For example, all of a community's arts are not equally appropriate for furthering God's goals at a given time. A particular dance might be too strongly associated with immoral or idolatrous activities. Wise believers in the community may feel that use of that dance could pull new Christ-followers back to their old behaviors. We believe that God will eventually reclaim everything for himself (see Matt 19:28). However, the Holy Spirit's leading and local believers' insights can guide decisions about specific artistic forms today. Don't force kingdom change.

"From all the world" refers to the thousands of ways people communicate artistically. We are limited human beings. We don't naturally recognize art forms that are new to us. We especially have problems identifying the art forms of foreign cultures. One goal of this manual is to broaden our vision to see all of the potential resources. We want to have more of God's view of the arts.

"For all of God's purposes" helps us remember that God does not limit his use of the arts to our categories. In Scripture we see many contexts for artistic communication: corporate adoration, teaching, warfare, celebration, ritual, correcting, individual growth, healing, confession, remembering, and many other purposes. We've created this manual to help ourselves think beyond familiar uses of the arts in liturgy.

> **Careful Contextualization[1]**
>
> When applying Scripture to a particular art form in its cultural context, we must seek wisdom from the Holy Spirit. These steps provide a wise approach based on much prayerful experience.
>
> - Gather information from and with locals about the forms and their current meanings.
> - Study biblical teachings and principles with local people that relate to the forms in question.
> - Evaluate with local people the meanings of local forms in light of the related biblical teachings.
> - Encourage local people, based on what they have learned in the process, to make their own decisions to accept, reject, or alter the forms to create an appropriate, contextualized practice.

Figure 1. Careful Contextualization[2]

What Are Arts?

In this manual, we treat the arts as special kinds of communication. Like all communication systems, the arts are connected to particular times, places, and social contexts. They have their own symbols, grammars, and internal structures. Learning the arts can be like learning a foreign language. For example, in Thai performance, a dancer must learn how to move her arms and neck and eyebrows to tell a story; other cultures don't place the same importance on arm, neck, and eyebrow movements for storytelling. No single artistic language communicates precisely across lines of time, place, and culture. To understand any art form, we have to interact with its practitioners and study it. Getting to know local artists and their arts is our first job.

---

2 Originally known as "critical contextualization," outlined in Paul G. Hiebert, *Anthropological Insights for Missionaries* (Grand Rapids, MI: Baker Book House Co., 1985), 183-92.

But artistic forms of communication differ from other kinds of communication in several important ways. First, artistic communication places more emphasis on form manipulation than everyday interactions do. For example, poetic speech may rely on patterns of sound and thought such as rhyme, assonance, and metaphor. A simple exchange of information will not rely on those patterns. Circling a drum while repeating a sequence of foot movements relies heavily on form, too. Simply walking from one place to another does not. Adopting the facial expressions of a mythical character draws on form to communicate. Allowing a person's face to remain at rest does not.

Second, the arts reveal their uniqueness as limited spheres of interaction. Artistic events have beginnings and endings (no matter how fluid). In between the beginning and the end of an artistic event, people interact in unusually patterned ways. Ethnomusicologist Ruth Stone describes artistic events as "set off and made distinct from the natural world of everyday life by the participants."[3]

In this manual, we help you use these and other characteristics to discover and describe artistic communication. We help you recognize it in any community you enter, including your own. We use broad discovery parameters, not wanting to miss any important communication that doesn't fit our existing categories. Our view of an artistic act might refer to a concert of Spanish flamenco, rehearsals for a Broadway musical, a painting hanging on a café wall, a father speaking a proverb to his daughter, or rhythmic wailing at a gravesite. Around the world, people use tens of thousands of kinds of artistic communication. The world too often undervalues these amazing resources.

 Discuss examples of arts in your community that outsiders might not understand.

How Do Arts and Culture Interact?

The arts may both reflect and influence the cultures in which they exist. Artistic communication reflects the shape of other aspects of culture, too. It's interwoven with the rest of life. For example, members of Kaluli society in Papua New Guinea use a metaphor "lift-up-over-sounding." The figure of speech appears in several aspects of their lives. The idea underlies music-making. Two singers alternate in taking the lead role. They produce interweaving layers of sound. A similar phenomenon occurs in Kaluli conversation. People "interrupt" each other. They are co-creating, "lifting-up-over" together. In this example, musical form reflects a widespread Kaluli communication pattern.[4]

Artistic communication can also change cultures. It has unique abilities to motivate people to action. It can inspire feelings of solidarity. It also provides socially acceptable space to disagree. One example comes from women in the African Apostolic Church in southern Africa. In a worship service, they can communicate their grievances against men. They are not allowed

---

3 Ruth Stone, "Communication and Interaction Processes in Music Events among the Kpelle of Liberia" (PhD diss., Indiana University, 1979), 37.

4 Steven Feld, "Sound Structure as Social Structure," *Ethnomusicology* 28, no. 3 (1984): 383–409.

to preach to a congregation, but women may interrupt a sermon with a song. The song may contain lyrics such as: "Men, stop beating your wives. Only then will you go to Heaven." Women-led songs provide symbolic protection for their critical content.[5] In this case, artistic communication has power to change other parts of culture. Arts may also strengthen existing power structures. National anthems represent clear examples of power structures strengthened with artistic communication.

What Is Creativity?

The purpose of this manual is to help you inspire artistic creativity that supports the expansion of God's kingdom. Understanding how creativity works is important. We describe it like this: artistic creativity occurs when one or more people produce a new event or work of enhanced communication. The new work has not previously existed in its exact form. The creators of the work use their personal skills, the social patterns of their culture, and symbolic systems to create the work. The newness of the event or work varies according to its basic parts and their degrees of originality. Each culture values newness in unique ways.

To understand how people in a culture create, find out who the creators are. Also, discover what skills, knowledge, and techniques they need to produce something new. For created works to enter a society's life, the gatekeepers must accept the works. A community's gatekeepers are the people who strongly influence the acceptance of an innovation. Learn who the gatekeepers are. Also, discover what restrictions or customs the new works might encounter. Who influences whether a group values, learns, and passes on a newly created work?

An important understanding of tradition underlies our approach to creativity. Tradition is not a fixed body of ideas and practices. Rather, one person is constantly passing tradition to another person. One generation is constantly passing tradition to the next generation. Every act of transmission introduces small or large changes. This manual helps you come alongside local creators in their communities. It helps you inspire moments of artistic activity that may become lasting traditions. Traditions endure when people remain motivated to transmit them. People maintain motivation when social structures and resources support their creativity. Food historian John Edge said, "Tradition is innovation that succeeds."[6]

Everyone who contributed to this manual can identify exceptionally gifted artists who inspired and motivated us. Sometimes gifted individuals see the world differently. Sometimes they feel compelled to play with and fundamentally change traditions. People who change traditions shift the standard. We want to encourage standard-shifters to create for God and his kingdom. Creating for God should enhance their contributions and creative

---

5 Bennetta Jules-Rosette, "Ecstatic Singing: Music and Social Integration in an African Church," in *More than Drumming: Essays on African and Afro-Latin American Music and Musicians*, ed. Irene V. Jackson (Westport, CT: Greenwood, 1985), 119–44.

6 John T. Edge, Twitter post, February 12, 2010, 6:49 A.M., http://twitter.com/johntedge/status/9009036481.

output because it connects them explicitly to the Ultimate Creator. Our focus in this manual, however, is creativity as a communal activity. We emphasize creativity that everyone contributes to. Consider this creed:

> In the beginning, God created:
> - Heaven and Earth,
> - day and night,
> - water and soil,
> - plants and animals, and
> - man and woman.
>
> God created ex nihilo (out of nothing).
> What wasn't, now was.
> And it was good.
> God made us in his image.
> One way we reflect this image is in our desire and ability to create.
>
> We make:
> - cities and dams,
> - houses and shops,
> - clothes and furniture, and
> - stories and songs and dances and masks.
>
> We create ex creatio—out of what God already made
> - every time we write a letter or an email,
> - when we greet or comfort someone,
> - when we cook a meal or play a game or dance, and
> - when we paint a portrait or sketch a cartoon.
>
> Every time we do something in a way that never existed before, for a purpose or context that doesn't exactly repeat a previous purpose or context . . . we are acting like God.
>
> But love compels us to: take one more step, to make disciples of sons and daughters, brothers and sisters, commission someone to write a song or a poem, or craft a chair, help someone translate the Bible into their language, tutor a refugee, or raise a child.
>
> Every time we inspire or prepare someone else to create, we are performing one of the highest, most satisfying and enduring acts of love.
>
> We are not God, but creativity flows through us.
>
> In that, we are like him.

1. List examples of ways in which you have been creative.
2. List examples of ways in which you have helped someone create.
3. Discuss examples of other things God has created.

Whom Do We Encourage?

Most people in the world speak more than one language. They also perform and experience music, dance, stories, and other arts from multiple traditions and geographical locations. Each community has a unique, changing blend of local, regional, national, and international artistic activity. Each individual within a community also has a unique mix of local, regional, national, and international artistic activity. How do you know where to join in? Your answer depends on two things: how your community fits into the historical spread of the church (mission) and your particular calling.

Three approaches to arts in mission

Historically, Christians have approached the spread of their faith in three ways: 1) **Bring It–Teach It**, 2) **Build New Bridges**, 3) and **Find It–Encourage It.**

Though the three approaches are distinct, they also interact in complex ways.

1) People working cross-culturally in the Bring It–Teach It framework bring their own arts to teach to the people in another community. In effect, they teach foreign art forms to local communities. Throughout church history, cross-cultural workers have practiced this approach. Today, it continues to happen. In rural Democratic Republic of Congo, I could sing the song "Ekangeneli Na Yesu" a week after I arrived. Previous missionaries produced "Ekangeneli Na Yesu" with Lingala language lyrics set to the tune of the Western song "Auld Lang Syne."

The Bring It–Teach It approach may result in a common artistic language that unifies people around the world. It also sometimes contributes to satisfying and pleasurable cultural blends. It brings an inspiring sense of mystery surrounding the worship of God. However, Bring It–Teach It also has frequent and dangerous downsides. It often results in miscommunication of emotions and messages. Communities see God as foreign to them. Local artists feel excluded or demoralized. Local communities sense that Christianity is irrelevant. Kingdom diversity is weakened.

2) People reaching out in the Build New Bridges approach learn enough about another community's arts to influence how they use their own arts in ministry. For example, art therapists have used local materials or songs to guide suffering children through a healing process. Build New Bridges could also include collaborations between artists of different cultures for common purposes. Then the resulting products have characteristics of more than one tradition.

The Build New Bridges model often requires only a short time for initial progress to occur. It works well in communities who are experiencing trauma. Traumatized communities often don't have energy or resources for their own artistic expression. Building New Bridges is a good option for communities without resources. It also promotes healthy interdependent relationships where everyone equally shares their arts. However, problems come when a significant power difference exists between the cross-cultural worker and the artists in the community. An outsider's higher social status can reduce local artists' resolve and courage. Building New Bridges may also produce unsustainable results. New, collaborative artistic production that is not deeply rooted in local traditions and social systems will likely fade away.

3) In Find It–Encourage It, the cross-cultural worker learns to know local artists and their arts. He or she learns in ways that encourage the artists to create in the forms they know best. You can think of the worker as an advocate for someone else's creativity. She helps give birth to new creations. The new creations flow organically from the community. The approach usually requires longer-term relationships with people than the other two approaches. It also requires an unending commitment to learning.

None of these three categories are untainted by earthly imperfection. However, we wrote *Creating Local Arts Together* for people working primarily in the third approach. We did this for two reasons. First, we see Jesus as our primary model. As King of the kingdom, he left his heavenly culture to become human. He learned to walk, talk, sing, and dress himself in an earthly, minority society for nearly thirty years. Then he entered his full ministry (Phil. 2). Like Jesus, we should be with local people, learn from them, and then give to them. Second, we believe the church is largely neglecting this approach in its mission strategies. The consequences of the neglect are often tragic.

Discuss examples you've seen of each of these three types of spreading the kingdom of God:
Bring It–Teach It, Build New Bridges, and Find It–Encourage It.

Your particular calling

We suggest three criteria to help you in your decisions about how to invest your limited gifts, time, and energies in a community.

First, ask God to show you where he's working. Remember that his voice might not be the loudest, most obvious voice.

Second, enter a discovery process with members of the community. Together you'll be wiser in knowing how and where to work. Your background and the approaches in this manual have produced valuable knowledge and experience in you. If you have submitted yourself to a locally led decision-making process, don't be afraid to humbly speak the truth from your perspective.

Third, give extra attention to local artists who represent older, geographically or ethnically rooted traditions. We encourage the focus on local artists because they have unique skills and knowledge. In many places their skills and knowledge are endangered. To thrive, communities need a combination of deeply rooted traditions and innovation. Our working definition of a local art is: an artistic form of communication that a community can create, perform, teach, and understand from within. Understanding includes knowing the artistic forms, meanings, language, and social context.

Societies connect through media and face-to-face interactions. Members of societies encounter each other by following their individual interests. However, contact also occurs in the context of social, financial, church, and other local and global influences. People are multilingual, multicultural, and multi-artistic. A community marked by the kingdom of God has members who reflect on the value and purposes of each artistic communication form. They work toward a combination of value and purpose that glorifies God.

Discuss ways that God might be working uniquely in your community.

Discuss particular gifts, skills, and experiences that God has developed in you.

Discuss how you think God wants you to approach the older traditions in your community.

Who Does What?

We wrote the manual for you, an arts advocate. You want to help members of a community—perhaps your own—integrate artistic action more fully into their lives. You want their temporal and eternal futures to be better. Your primary job is to help others make new things in genres they already know. If you are an artist, you may need to find outlets to express your own gifts. Expressing your own gifts is a great thing. Your primary job, however, is to help others make new artistic things. This manual will help you help others.

The whole process of artistic co-creation requires people with many kinds of competencies, knowledge, and skills. Below are some of the needed skills:

- artistic sensibilities and abilities,
- cultural research capabilities,
- relationships with all parts of local, regional, and national communities,
- planning and organizing skills,
- communication skills appropriate to different contexts, and
- technical competencies for recording and production.

No one person or type of person can do everything required for Creating Local Arts Together. That's why we put "together" and "we" and other plural terms in so many sentences in this manual. We guide you through what needs to be done. We don't say who should do it.

We have two kinds of arts advocates in mind. The first group comprises those who are planning to spend a long time ministering in a community. They want a guide to beginning, planning, and implementing work that draws on local arts. We expect that they will eventually use most of the manual. Other people have only a short amount of time or energy for strengthening artists in a community. They can skim the manual and find something helpful. We've given a few time-saving ideas in "If You Don't Have Much Time" at the end of this chapter. We've written most of the manual with cross-cultural workers in mind. But it is also useful for people working in their own communities.

Whatever category you're in, our goal is to help you integrate artistic communication into a community's life. We assume that you have access to people and organizations that can help you do this. The people and organizations should have the basic skills, resources, and knowledge to work toward God's goals in a situation. For example, we don't include guidelines for deciding whether you should help start a literacy program. We don't give instructions on how to make a primer. Rather, we show how to use the lyrics of a local song style to aid in teaching reading. We demonstrate how local dances can play important roles in motivating people to learn to read. We offer tools to understand local visual patterns to incorporate into primer drawings. As another example, we don't develop a theological framework or methodology for starting new churches. Instead, we lead you through a process of getting to know local artists. We help you include their insights and skills into existing church-planting efforts.

Prepare Yourself

If you are new to a community, you probably don't have the skills to create or compose a new work in one of its artistic genres. Your contributions to the creative process will likely be in helping community members discover motivations to create. You may help design events and contexts in which skilled people create. You might help communities critique what their artists produce. You can also help people integrate new forms of lasting creativity into their lives. You may learn an artistic tradition well enough to make new works in it. As a result, your learning can have a profound effect on community members' motivation to create.[7] More than that, however, we want to help you enter into relationships with people in a community. We want your relationships to result in local artists creating new examples of existing genres. We want the new works to support a deepening of God's kingdom.

What experiences and gifts do you have that you can apply to this process?

What experiences and gifts will have to come from other people?

What might your role(s) be in a CLAT process?

---

[7] Read about Tom Avery's work with the Canela people of Brazil in *Worship and Mission for the Global Church: An Ethnodoxology Handbook* (2013, William Carey Library), Jack Popjes, "Now We Can Speak to God–in Song," chpt. 73.

How to Use This Manual

A flexible guide

We've organized the Creating Local Arts Together process as numbered steps because each step flows logically into the next. Often, however, the steps won't follow this specific order. In fact, each step might reveal a need for doing more of one of the others. For example, to improve a newly crafted story, the community members may need to go back and do more research on poetic features of good local stories. This may require performing activities in the analyze step. Ideally, you and members of the community are trying ideas, and then learning from what happens. You are then doing more research, trying again, and continuing the process: act and reflect, reflect and act. This pattern results in healthy, growing creativity. Think of the steps as a reliable, solid framework you can refer to. Do not think of the steps as etched in stone. And again, think of the steps as seven conversations you need to have in order to increase the likelihood of success.

Another warning about this ordered presentation is that some steps include elements of other steps. Most importantly, the activities you develop in Step 5 that spark (or inspire) the creation of new works are bundles of several steps. For example, a workshop about weaving cloth with scriptural marriage advice may include analyzing, sparking, improving, and integrating. Our emphasis is not on rigidly defining and requiring separate steps. We emphasize helping community members make sure that they've included each component somewhere in the big picture of their lives. Please see the accompanying Ethnodoxology Handbook and Manual website for more resources (www.ethnodoxologyhandbook.com).

Features of this manual

Throughout the manual, you'll see "First Glance" activities. Artistic communication is frustratingly complex, so sometimes, knowing how to start an analysis feels impossible. We designed the "First Glance" tools to give you a quick idea of the most important elements to consider. Then we show you how to go deeper.

You'll also notice specially marked or formatted content. The following icons indicate the text that follows is an activity that you can perform:

A block of shaded content marks especially important content that you will want to refer to more than once.

Some Advice and Encouragement

Discuss the clat process with leaders

You should discuss the CLAT process with leaders representing your connections to the community. If you are part of an external organization partnering with the community, all leaders involved need to understand the goals and process described in this manual. Perhaps you can arrange a special meeting to describe the CLAT process.

Research all the time

Learning to know someone else deeply is a fundamental act of love. It is also necessary for success in everything you do. So whenever you're not sure what to do, go ask a question, practice a dance, or observe an event. All of these things help you learn. Research equals learning equals love. When we research a community, we learn about it. When we learn about a community, we demonstrate love for its members.

Sometimes your research will take you into realms of belief and practice that contradict your Christian faith. In these cases, adopt an attitude of "temporary suspension of disbelief." Do not act counter to what God wants you to do. At the same time, try to identify with your friends, at least momentarily. This issue can be tough, so pray fervently.

It's (almost) all about relationships

Our first priority is whole human beings. We do not want only to learn others' art forms, so build relationships. Get permission to do things. Earn the right to ask questions. Respect local limitations on what you can do (for example, don't expect to study female initiation rites if you're a man). Most of the time, your authentic, reciprocal relationships with people will allow you to enter their lives. Other times you will benefit from others' long-term relationships with the community to assist your own connections. In any case, always remember that although we care deeply about the artistic life of people, we also emphasize that they are people first.

What if they don't want it?

Even if you do everything in this manual perfectly, humbly, and respectfully (which nobody can do), you will almost certainly run into resistance. Resistance could come from several sources. A community might have a low opinion of artists. Theological or ideological arguments might go against certain kinds of arts being used in certain contexts. Previous negative experiences with trying to do new things with arts might create negative feelings. Inertia from longstanding traditions could also impact resistance. Underappreciation of the importance and transformative potential of artistic communication could have an effect as well. Our whole approach of creating together within a community should mitigate much of this, but it won't remove all problems. The following bits of counsel may help you navigate your way with more success and peace.

First, protect, pray for, love, and encourage the artists you work with. Whenever they create something for a public space, they become vulnerable to negative cultural forces. Second, as much as possible, work through existing authority structures. This may not always work, because arts sometimes present uncomfortable truth to power. However, sustainability offers many benefits if community leaders are willing to listen. Third, you may want to start small with a pilot project. Work to help create a few examples of local artistic genres for kingdom purposes. Then present them to community leaders. The presentation to leaders can be a crucial step in opening a door to further creativity. Fourth, be both likeable and persistent in your relationships. Fifth, don't be afraid of trying and failing. Nurture your own humility. Know that God's plan for you and a community will never be exactly what you think. Sixth and finally, talk with God a lot. He'll tell you what you need to know, because it's his kingdom. Remember: "If any of you lacks wisdom, you should ask God, who gives generously to all without finding fault, and it will be given to you" (Jas1:5).

Whenever possible, help leaders plan for the arts

One of the most common reasons that communities and organizations don't integrate their arts into their work is that they don't plan for it. You can help solve this problem. You can learn the processes through which leaders in churches, nongovernmental organizations (NGOs), and other groups interacting with a community make decisions. Then, graciously ask to join those processes in appropriate ways and at key moments. Prepare yourself well. Be ready to offer concrete suggestions for how people can use the great resources of their community's arts to reach their goals.

Planning can be very important for long-term integration of kingdom creativity in a community. In fact, our seven Creating Local Arts Together steps themselves constitute a planning method. You can relate the seven steps directly to other methods. You may be working with an organization that has adopted a particular planning system. If you are, adapt vocabulary we've developed in the manual to their system. Then use their vocabulary in your conversations.

One warning is that regardless of how much you and a community plan, God often works in ways we can't anticipate. You should plan—but always be aware of individuals or groups who might be responding to something unexpected that God is doing. Enjoy being surprised.

You can't do it all, but you can do enough

Since the beginning of human existence, people have been integrating arts into their communities in astounding ways. They haven't had the help of this manual. Sometimes, individuals and communities create arts with no explicit purpose in mind, simply saying, "I really want/need to do this!" Sometimes those bits of artistry spread and enliven the kingdom of God in completely unpredictable and positive ways. So you may not have to do any of this.

Most communities, though, will benefit from the manual. Every community and its artistic forms of communication represent an unfathomable degree of complexity and variation. Even the most accomplished master of an art form can learn more and increase his or her skills. To make matters more difficult, the physical and social contexts of communities are constantly changing. Sometimes the changes are dramatic. In short, you could never fully perform all of the activities we describe in this manual. Even if you just studied one art form, you would run out of time. You cannot possibly do everything.

But you can do enough.

Insights from academic fields like ethnomusicology, performance studies, anthropology, linguistics, missiology, and neuroscience show us that we can understand the important patterns of human artistic communication. God's view of his final kingdom encompasses every language and nation (Rev 7). We can know each other. However, because of the complexity of communities, our interactions with them are more like explorations and adventures than scientific processes. Use this manual to sharpen and broaden your understanding of artistic communication in the kingdom of God. But don't try to do everything. Explore what seems most relevant and productive.

If you don't have much time

You may not always have the time or resources to commit to the thorough process we describe in this manual. Maybe you're not sure how to begin the process. This brief section contains suggestions for arts activities that require little preparation. These activities will get you started and will encourage more complete actions when you have more time. No artistic exploration or encouragement is ever wasted.

To start, look for natural connections you may have with local artists. You might be intrigued by a particular art form—you just like it. You may have experience or skills related to an art form such as dance or weaving. You may have a personal affinity with a practitioner of an art form. Whatever the case, remember that ultimately you want to get to know and encourage people involved in local arts. Look for ways to make relationships. If you can only do one thing, ask an artist to teach you something.

> **SIMPLE ARTS ENGAGEMENT ACTIVITIES**
>
> - Make an initial list of local art forms, using the "Take a First Glance at a Community's Arts" activity in Step 1.
> - Attend artistic events and describe them briefly in a notebook.
> - Collect instruments.
> - Transcribe song texts.
> - Do language and culture learning with artists. Spend relaxed social time with them.
> - Make systematic audio or video recordings of an art form according to song categories, composers, events in a village, or proverbs.
> - Learn to play an instrument, sing, dance, act, weave, or tell a story in a local genre.
> - Talk about these things with local friends and colleagues:
>   - How did the arts in the community originate? Who created the things people use or perform?
>   - What are people's general attitudes toward people involved in different local art forms? Positive? Negative?
>   - Are there parts of a performance that have special symbolic significance? For example, colors, shapes, instruments, or clothes?
>   - How does the way people do local art forms now differ from how they did them in the past? Are young people learning how to do them? How does someone become good at them?
>   - Are there certain art forms that only men or only women or only children can do?
>   - How do people feel when they're involved in different local art forms? Do they ever enter into ecstatic states?
>   - How are local art forms connected to religious beliefs?
>   - What artistic expressions in the culture are not currently being used in the worship of God? Why? How might God want to redeem one for a purpose in his kingdom?

Figure 2. Simple Arts Engagement Activities

Ultimate Motivations: A Note on Heaven & Hell

We have invoked signs of the kingdom of God as a central motivation for using this manual. We want God's people everywhere to act in artistic ways that result in more evidence of Heaven on Earth. So far, however, we have barely mentioned the first sign of the kingdom of God in communities: the first sign is each human being's existence. God created people in his image. The existence of every child, woman, and man is a fact that points to God's home, Heaven. How should this fundamental sign influence our work?

The answer to this question depends in part on our belief that eternity exists in two distinct forms: Heaven and Hell. Heaven is associated with the Trinitarian God—the Father, Jesus, and the Holy Spirit—and all that is good. Hell is associated with Satan and all that is evil. On Earth, these realities become complex and confusing. Adolph Hitler brilliantly developed his oratorical gifts. His speeches moved and excited people in invigorating, pleasurable ways. His creative skills dimly reflected the creative skills of God. But Hitler used his gifts in violent ways, causing horror, hopelessness, despair, and agony.

The negative effects dimly reflected Satan's cruel desires. We believe that the realities of Heaven and Hell are infinitely more extreme than we imagine, both on Earth and after.

These truths leave us with a few lessons. First, we must approach every person and his or her gifts as infinitely valuable. One man who travels a lot sometimes finds that new stimuli from clothes, hairstyles, skin tones, sounds, or smells elicit negative responses in his mind. When this happens, he repeats to himself, "Image of God! Image of God!" Each person carries God's mark. Our first attitudes toward people should always be generous and humble. We should expect goodness and beauty. Second, we should study Heaven and Hell biblically, meditatively, and imaginatively. When we know these realities more physically, intellectually, and emotionally, we can discern more. Third, we can't allow ourselves to believe that the pain and joy of Earth is all that exists. If we do, we might settle for simply alleviating hunger. We might not care whether someone connects the satisfaction of eating with the Creator of food.

Finally, we should encourage the spread of all types of signs of the kingdom. They are all good in themselves. But we can never forget that people need to know the source of all good: Father-Jesus-Spirit. We can ask God to nurture our understandings of both Heaven and Hell. Both can motivate us powerfully.

 **Spend some time praying about the topics below. If possible, pray using artistic languages–painting, drawing, dancing, acting, singing, storytelling, or some other form you know.**

 **Listen to God, then respond to him. Communicate with him about the things that excite you most in these discussions, then about the things that frighten or worry you most.**

 **Recall times or events in your life that were important in bringing you to this point in your life, especially as it concerns your involvement with arts in the kingdom of Heaven.**

Creating Local Arts Together (CLAT)

Figure 3 represents the method that this manual will lead you and a community through. The method is a continual process of researching and creating together. It results in more signs of God's kingdom. We call the process "Creating Local Arts Together" (sometimes shortened to the acronym CLAT) or "Co-creation." The people in the middle of Figure 3 represent community members performing in an artistic event.

The event is central to the whole process. It ensures that the community's efforts are grounded in a local reality. Community members know artists and their arts in context. The artistic event serves as the focus for seven steps:

1. **Meet** a Community and Its Artistic Genres
2. **Specify** Kingdom Goals
3. **Connect** Genres to Goals

4. **Analyze** Genres and Events
5. **Spark** Creativity
6. **Improve** Results
7. **Celebrate** and Integrate for Continuity

Finally, the people at the center of the whole process emphasize that learning and love should permeate and energize everything you do. In fact, you can think of these seven steps as seven conversations. Fundamentally, this manual is about helping other people make new artistic things.

Figure 3. Creating Local Arts Together

We now want to prepare you for the Creating Local Arts Together process. We will briefly introduce each step with a short illustrative story. In the early 1990s, Brian Schrag and his family lived in northwestern Democratic Republic of Congo (then Zaire). The Schrags were helping a community translate the Bible into their local Mono language. Brian will describe each component of the co-creation process. Then he will explain how each component fits into the Mono community's CLAT process.

Step 1: Meet a Community and Its Artistic Genres

The meet component involves getting to know basic information about a community. First, meeting means making relationships with people. Then it includes listing the kinds of arts that run through the community.

> ***Meeting a Mono Community and Its Artistic Genres.*** When we first moved to the village of Bili in Congo, I noticed that church members sang songs in a trade language, not in Mono. Some of the songs were translations of European and American hymns. Some were

composed in a national pop style. Outside the church, people played and sang very different kinds of music. They played and sang in the Mono language. Before we could encourage creativity, we needed to know more. I asked the leaders of a local church if we could meet under the paillote (straw-roofed gazebo) near our house. I wanted us to talk about their art forms and the Bible. Together, we made a list of twelve social contexts in which Mono people traditionally make music and dance. These contexts include social dances, rites of passage, personal expression, and giving counsel on the kundi (a local harp)—a performance genre called gbaguru.

Step 2: Specify Kingdom Goals

Which goals for a more Heaven-like life does the community want to work toward at this time? We've placed these signs of the kingdom into several broad categories: Identity and Sustainability, Shalom, Justice, Scripture, Church Life, and Personal Spiritual Life. However, this guide is just a beginning. Thousands, even tens of thousands, of signs of the kingdom of God exist. So act freely. Specify new signs of the kingdom. Create new activities that strengthen the signs. Tell and write stories of how artistic communication has spread. Share how it has deepened the kingdom of God.

> ***Specifying with a Mono Community.*** Still under the paillote, the pastor and elders discussed the many purposes of music evident in the Bible. They talked about the fact that God created every person in his image. They said that they didn't use Mono instruments in their church because early evangelists warned against local instrument use. Fifty years earlier, the first evangelists had counseled them to burn all physical objects associated with their traditional life. Based on Scripture, the leaders decided that God did want them to reclaim their music for his purposes. God's purposes included corporate worship. The people wanted to relate to God in new, deeper ways. They were curious about new possibilities.

Step 3: Connect Genres to Goals

After members of the community have chosen a goal, you can decide together which effects, art forms, content, and events will best support the goal.

> ***Connecting with a Mono Community.*** The leaders wanted Christians to understand Scripture better. They wanted Christians to value Mono traditions. They thought the familiarity of a church meeting was the best environment to experience something new for the first time. They also decided that gbaguru was the best genre. Much of the Bible is about communicating wisdom, and the gbaguru genre offers counsel. Therefore, the leaders believed they could incorporate gbaguru well into worship.

Step 4: Analyze Genres and Events

Creating something in an existing artistic genre for new purposes requires a great deal of knowledge, skill, and wisdom. Your first impressions of an art form new to you are usually wrong and always incomplete. Step 4 helps you get to the details of art forms and their meanings, thus increasing your understanding. Knowing the details of artistic form and meaning will help the community, and you, identify artistic elements that will penetrate the community for the kingdom.

> ***Analyzing Genres and Events with a Mono Community.*** Spurred by my own interests, I had already started to learn about the kundi. It is used to perform gbaguru songs. I asked who the best kundi player was, and everyone pointed me to Punayima Kanyama. In this case, I analyzed Punayima performing in the gbaguru genre at several events. I video-recorded him. I transcribed melodies, lyrics, and fingerings. Punayima also taught me to play a couple of songs. Learning to play the songs deepened my insight into the forms and themes of the genre. For instance, I learned that gbaguru lyrics usually contain Mono proverbs. I discovered performances are usually by men. Vocal melodies usually follow the tonal patterns of the words in the lyrics. Lastly, composers usually require time alone to make new songs.

Step 5: Spark Creativity

One sparks (or inspires) creativity by performing an act that results in a new bit of artistry developing. You may spark creativity by simply suggesting that someone carve a new mask or compose a new song for a celebration. Sometimes, inspiring creativity may require more complex and time-consuming activities. Examples of more complex activities are workshops, commissions, apprenticeships, and festivals. Local artists may also develop a new version of an existing ritual or ceremony. Whatever activity is chosen, be sure to include all people who are interested in integrating new works into the community. Also include community leaders who control the integration of new works into the community.

> ***Sparking with a Mono Community.*** In the Mono community, I asked who could compose new Scripture-based gbaguru songs for corporate worship. Because the first evangelists told new Mono Christians to burn their instruments, nobody in the church knew how to play the kundi. After some discussion, the leaders decided that they would choose some church people to learn as apprentices from a kundi master. We met weekly. Punayima taught us how to construct a kundi and how to tune it. Then he taught us to play some simple songs.

Step 6: Improve Results

Evaluation for improvement is essential to the co-creative process. We want community members to integrate creativity into their lives. We want the creativity to truly result in communities achieving their spiritual, social, and physical goals. Evaluation according to agreed-upon criteria helps community members make their imperfect artistic communication more effective.

Improving with a Mono Community. Unfortunately, we didn't evaluate the early songs that Punayima and others created. They could have been even better. However, we included processes to improve Scripture-based songs that Mono people have composed since then. Bible translators checked for scriptural accuracy and clarity. And Mono musical experts checked that the songs were excellent examples of the genres they represented.

Step 7: Celebrate and Integrate for Continuity

Our desire is that community members will increasingly integrate kingdom creativity into their daily, weekly, monthly, and yearly lives. To do this, they need to teach newly created artworks to others. They need a plan to continue creating. At the simplest level, workshops or commissioning should include teaching times for attendees. They should also include planning time for teaching new works to wider audiences in the future. A good idea is first to teach a small group and get feedback with evaluation questions. Then present the works to a larger group.

Celebrating and Integrating with a Mono Community. Somewhere during our apprenticeship, the other students decided to form a kundi group, called Chorale Ayo (the Love Choir). Punayima composed a song about God creating man and woman from the Earth. When we played and sang the song in a church service, the normally energetic congregation was still and silent. I feared that we had somehow made a mistake, maybe causing people to think of old gods. So after the service, I asked a friend why everyone was so quiet. His reply was, "What could we do? The song cut our hearts." This meant that it touched their emotions, minds, and wills in deep ways unique to their own arts.

The Chorale Ayo continued to sing in congregational meetings. Some of the apprentices began to compose their own songs. Then war and personal calamities interrupted Mono life. After a long break, similar kundi groups emerged in other villages. One part of the Mono community—the Protestant church—was celebrating good parts of their traditions more. But I wanted to include more people. We were planning a big fête (a celebration) marking the completion of our newly built village house. I had the idea to commission songs to be performed at the event. Two songs were in traditional Mono genres. On the night of our celebration, hundreds of people from all social classes experienced Jesus's teachings in familiar Mono forms. The songs included Jesus's parable of the wise and foolish builders (Matt 7:24-27).

CREATING LOCAL ARTS TOGETHER (CLAT): A SUMMARY

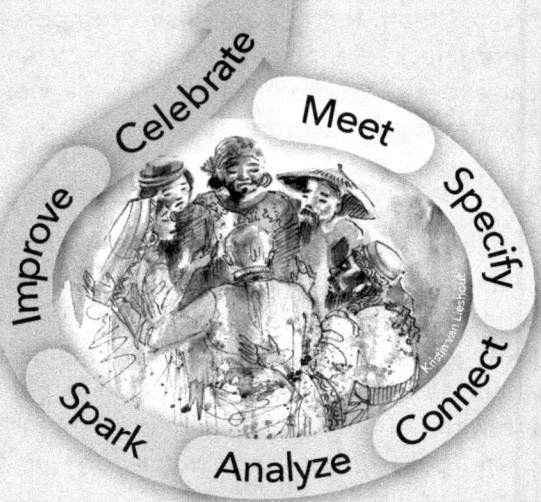

The CLAT process shows how to help communities draw on their arts to bring about God's kingdom goals in that community. There are seven basic steps to Creating Local Arts Together. You can also think about them as seven conversations. Research supports it all, emphasizing the need to be a learner at all times. The steps are:

Meet a Community and Its Artistic Genres
Explore artistic and social resources that exist in the community.

Specify Kingdom Goals
Discover the kingdom goals that the community wants to work toward.

Connect Genres to Goals
Community chooses an artistic genre and activities that can help it meet its goals.

Analyze Genres and Events
Describe the event as a whole. Describe its artistic forms as arts. Describe the forms in relationship to broader cultural context. Detailed knowledge of the art forms is crucial to sparking (inspiring) creativity. It is important for improving what is produced, and it is necessary for integrating new works into the community.

Spark Creativity
Community implements activities to inspire creativity within the genres and events they have chosen.

Improve Results
Community evaluates results of the sparking activities and makes them better.

Celebrate and Integrate for Continuity
Plan and implement ways that this new kind of creativity can continue. Identify more contexts where the new and old arts can be displayed and performed.

Figure 4. Creating Local Arts Together (CLAT): A Summary

STEP 1

MEET A COMMUNITY AND ITS ARTISTIC GENRES

Step 1 is discovering and describing a community and its arts. When you start to work with a community, observation (research) is very important. You want to find out as much as you can about the community and the community's arts. Art comes from its context, so knowing about a community will help you understand its art.

What community are you targeting? We define a community this way: a community shares a story of events, characters, and ideas that have occurred in its past. Everyone knows and can refer to the past events, characters, and ideas. These shared experiences give the community members a reason to keep gathering together. A community also shares an identity. Markers of this identity distinguishes the group from other communities. Identity markers may be language, food, dress, religion, or shared struggles. Communities also share interaction patterns. Examples of shared interaction patterns include rituals, festivals, family living quarters, visual and tactile symbols and patterns, and many more.

Communities share a story, an identity, and a way of interacting. But always remember that communities change. They are made up of individuals who come and go, make their own decisions, and respond differently to the many situations they encounter.

As you begin exploring your community, write down all your discoveries in one place. A Community Arts Profile (CAP) will help you do this. A Community Arts Profile (CAP) is a database or document where you keep all the information on the community and its arts (see pp. 51-53).

Take a First Glance at a Community

A quick look at a community will help you understand the context for developing and performing art. Art does not exist alone. Get initial information about the community's geographical location, language, identity markers, and communication methods.

Decide on the range of your research. Will you study one clan in a village, or everyone in a region who speaks the same language? Describe things from as many viewpoints as possible. The chart below is a question guide. You can get information in other ways, too:

- Ask friends, leaders, and other contacts from the community to show you other resources, including people.
- Read and observe how community members have presented themselves in books, articles, videos, recordings, and other media.
- Read academic research, encyclopedias, and other resources to see what others have said about the community.

 Write down a preliminary description of the community you want to work with. Include these topics: where they are; how many they are and what they are like; what story and identity they share; how the community has changed over time.

STUDYING THE COMMUNITY: SOME QUESTIONS TO ASK

Where is the community and how many people comprise it? This includes basic information like village or town, province, and nation.

What ties the community together? Answers could include factors like language, geography, ethnic identity, and social structure.

How do they communicate with each other and how often? This question involves languages and modes of communication, such as face-to-face, telephone, and electronic social media.

How did they get there? Identify important historical events and patterns that have brought the community to its geographical location and affected its identity.

Figure 5. Studying the Community: Some Questions to Ask

Take a First Glance at a Community's Arts

We help communities create from artistic resources that they already possess. Using resources already in existence is a core component of our approach. So one of the first things to do is to make a list of existing arts.

Finding and recognizing artistic genres

Every community has a unique catalog of types of arts, and each community puts unique meanings on each type of art. Your categories of arts will probably not match those of any community you work with. So how do you find them? Fortunately, there are some common characteristics of arts around the world that help us in our research.

Step 1

The first commonality is that cultures often celebrate important events and transitions with artistic communication. Events to look at include life cycle and historical events, activities, ceremonies, and nature. If you can identify rituals and special events that exist in a community, you can find out about the arts that are associated with those events.

The second common feature of arts is that they are special kinds of communication that are more stylized than other kinds of communication. Notice when people move in special patterns (dance), sing, act, paint, speak with rhythms or rhymes, or do something in a special performance setting (like on a stage). These characteristics probably point you to artistic genres. The "Make a Quick List of Artistic Genres" activity uses these unique characteristics of arts to get started.

> **HOW TO RECOGNIZE ARTISTIC COMMUNICATION ACTS**
>
> **Arts may have a distinctive performance context**
> The artistic event is set off from everyday occurrences by such things as time of day, place, language, participants, and so on.
>
> **Arts may expand or contract the density of information**
> Certain kinds of poetry, for example, convey a great deal in just a few words. Other forms of artistic expression expand the information through space, music, and repetition.
>
> **Arts may assume more or special knowledge**
> Sometimes terminology or alternative meanings of words are specific to a particular artistic genre.
>
> **Arts exhibit special formal structure**
> Artistic expressions are often limited by constraints of form which are not relevant to everyday communication.
>
> **Arts may elicit unusual responses**
> Artistic expressions often produce a strong emotional or physical response from people who experience them.
>
> **Arts may require unusual expertise**
> Artistic expressions often seem to take specialized training to perform; not everyone can do them.

Figure 6. How to Recognize Artistic Communication Acts

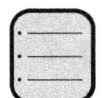

Make a Quick List of Artistic Genres

To make an initial list of artistic genres, gather a few people from a community and ask them questions like this:

- When do people in this community sing? play instruments? dance? tell stories? act? carve? paint? use their bodies in unusual ways? play games? build special structures? Remember that each culture divides up and talks about its forms of artistic communication in unique ways, so learn its vocabulary.

- Do people in this community do anything special surrounding the birth of a child? someone's death? someone's passage from childhood to adulthood? For each affirmative answer, ask them to describe what special things happen and make note of the arts involved.

Whenever an artistic genre comes up in discussion, jot down a few of the genre's basic characteristics:

- Local name and brief description
- People involved (men, women, youth, children, specialists, a particular socioeconomic group, etc.)
- When it's usually done (events, particular days, seasons, months, times of day, etc.)
- Connotations and associations (celebration, fertility, worship, death, etc.)
- Effects on participants (pride in identity; feelings of solidarity, lust, fear, or courage; motivation to act; remember life-crucial information, etc.)
- Institutions or organizations that are associated with the genre (church, government office, community group, club, etc.)

Don't worry about getting all the details while you're making a survey. You can add more information as you keep learning.

 **Put Basic Facts About Genres into a Chart for Comparison**

In Step 3, community members will evaluate each genre for use in reaching kingdom goals. This chart will help them do that. Start it now, then add more information as needed. Figure 7 shows a chart with data from Mono arts (DR Congo).

Genre	Brief Description	Event	Participants	Connotations	Effects	Institutions
gaza aga	male circumcision dance	male circumcision rites	young men	war	teach to fight, give courage	Ngakoala–Mono judges
Nzembo na Nzambe	European hymns translated into Lingala	church meetings	church members	faith, belief, missionaries	solidarity	Protestant church
gbaguru	wisdom songs	private contexts	harp player/singer, listeners	wisdom, counsel	motivation to act wisely	none
Nganga	songs for Zhugwa, god of the hunt	while hunting	Hunters	Zhugwa	give courage, hope for success	none
agbolo	children's game songs	where children play	Children	fun, freedom	pleasure, solidarity	none

Figure 7. Sample Mono (DR Congo) Genre Comparison Chart

Start Exploring the Community's Social and Conceptual Life

Developing a broad understanding of the community is important, and a broad understanding of the community comes through anthropological study. Research topics especially helpful to understanding a community's arts include these: how people use languages; how they relate to each other in social groups, especially family; how people get what they need to live (for example, food, shelter, health, education); differences in status or power between people; religious beliefs and activities; and worldview. Wide research in these areas is beyond the scope of this manual. Learn to do this kind of research, or find somebody else who can.

Continue Your Research

You will never completely understand all there is to know about a community, so you have to keep learning. Some of the best ways to learn have been developed by anthropologists, and you can learn how to do them. These include learning by watching while doing (participant-observation), by doing (learning an art foreign to you), by asking (interviews), by writing (note-taking), by capturing and viewing audio and video (recording), and by taking photographs. Find somebody to teach you these skills, through classes, books, or apprenticeship.

Finally, we want all our interactions with people to be guided by love. In all your research, be loving, humble, generous, and desire the best for your community.

STEP 2

SPECIFY KINGDOM GOALS

Our goal as followers of Christ is to see God's kingdom revealed on Earth. We want to see his kingdom lived as fully as possible on Earth, but we know that we will only experience God's kingdom fully in Heaven. All communities want a better life in some way. Community members are often striving toward the kingdom of God without knowing that's what they are doing. You can help them on this journey. The term "kingdom goals" helps us see the many ways God can be revealed on Earth.

In Step 2, we first present a brief summary of some of the ways God can be revealed. Then we lead you through a process of helping a community decide what goal(s) they want to work toward.

 **For each category of kingdom goals below,**
1) give an example that reflects that goal, and
2) suggest other kinds of kingdom goals.

Category of Kingdom Goals: Identity & Sustainability

Valuing Identity
Where the kingdom of God thrives, communities value their cultures.

In many places, minority group members think more highly of other people than they think of themselves. They belittle the usefulness, beauty, or intrinsic value of their own culture. Yet "God created human beings in his own image" (Gen 1:27 NLT).

People valuing the good aspects of their societies is right, healthy, and holy. The more a community's members appropriately value their own culture, the more the kingdom of God is likely to thrive. Further, a community's artistic genres represent some of the most identifiable and valuable parts of its culture. If community members see no good in their own arts, they will not use their arts to worship God or to communicate truth to each other. We want to explore ways that a community can affirm its artistic resources. Then we aim to discover methods for creating new works that foster strong, godly cultural identity.

Teaching Children
Where the kingdom of God thrives, communities teach their traditions to their children.

One sign of a community's healthy identity is that the community's members teach good parts of their culture to their children and grandchildren. Identifying patterns of how each generation is passing on artistic knowledge, and what that knowledge is, will reveal a community's health.

Using Media
Where the kingdom of God thrives, communities contribute to local, regional, and global media channels.

People around the world are constantly figuring out new ways to communicate with each other. Communities whose members have an appropriately strong sense of their own value receive and learn artistic communication from others. They also contribute to available artistic resources through recordings of their own arts through local, regional, and global media.

Category of Kingdom Goals: Shalom

Jesus entered human society so that his followers would be able to live life to the fullest (John 10:10). He came so that his followers would have peace (John 14:27). The Hebrew word shalom represents much of what he promised: a state of peace, completeness, social harmony, justice, and health. Bryant Myers suggests that while "shalom and abundant life are ideals that we will not see this side of the second coming, the vision of a shalom that leads to life in its fullness is a powerful image that must inform and shape our understanding of any better human future."[8]

Healing
Where the kingdom of God thrives, communities respond to problems with healing and restoration.

The forces arrayed against shalom are frightening: war, natural disasters, sexual exploitation, disease, slavery, hunger, and thirst. A community that demonstrates characteristics of God's kingdom has community members who respond to these problems with healing and restoration. Artistic activity plays crucial roles in increasing shalom. It points suffering people to hope, instills solidarity within a community, and aids emotional and physical healing.

---

8 Bryant L. Myers, *Walking with the Poor: Principles and Practices of Transformational Development* (Maryknoll, NY: Orbis, 1999), 51.

Reconciliation
Where the kingdom of God thrives, communities reconcile with each other and with outside communities.

Artistic communication helps us open our arms to each other. It creates a feeling of unity that draws on something deeper than our histories. Singing and dancing together require individuals to unite in coordinated sound and movement. The resulting joy, pleasure, and solidarity establish new trust. They lift our eyes from our hurt to divine truths. Artistic forms of communication lead to powerful moments of repentance, forgiveness, solidarity, love, and lasting reconciliation.

Category of Kingdom Goals: Justice

Social Justice
Where the kingdom of God thrives, communities love and strengthen the poor and others on the margins.

God has communicated clearly and repeatedly throughout Scripture that he cares for people who are powerless. He highlights orphans, widows, and foreigners (Deut 10:18; Jas 1:27) and people without enough money (Deut 15:7-8; Ps 9:18; Luke 4:18, 6:20). He focuses on the politically and socially oppressed (Neh 9:15; Luke 1:46-55), prisoners (Ps 146:7), and hungry and homeless people (Isa 58:6-11; Matt 25:34-40). Jesus made a special point of telling the poor that they could have the kingdom of God (Luke 6:20-26). God shows how the insensitivity and sin of powerful people often produce injustice for marginalized people (Ps 12:5; 35:10; 72:12-14; Prov 22:22-23; Isa 10:1-3).

In response to these realities, God told people with resources to be generous (Deut 15:7-8; Prov 11:24-25; Rom 12:13; 2 Cor 9:6-13; Jas 2:15-17). He said to be kind to the marginalized (Prov 14:31), to defend them (Prov 31:8-9), and to break the systems that keep them down (Isa 58:6-11). Communities can work toward kingdom justice by drawing on their arts. They can instill hope, speak unwelcome truth to those in power, and encourage solidarity.

Education
Where the kingdom of God thrives, community members learn what they need to know to succeed in and contribute to their societies.

Unhealthy communities whose members do not value their identity often have weak educational systems. Rapid social change can leave people without the knowledge or training to flourish. The arts are powerful communication systems. For this reason, communities can include the arts in all educational subjects and teaching contexts.

Literacy
Where the kingdom of God thrives, communities read and listen to the Bible and other literature.

A community that demonstrates characteristics of God's kingdom has access to Scripture and other literature through written and aural means. People who can read, write, and listen are needed. Literacy goals relate to technical issues (for example, understanding language structure) and social issues (for example, wanting to read and write in a language and feeling capable of acquiring these skills). Artistic forms with significant language components (songs, drama, storytelling, proverbs, and riddles) and those without (dance, visual arts) will strengthen literacy goals.

Economic Opportunity
Where the kingdom of God thrives, all community members can work to contribute to the group's material well-being.

Scripture shows that humans are meant to work. God created the universe (Gen 1). Then he put Adam in charge of the garden of Eden (Gen 2:15). God advised Adam and Eve to be productive (Prov 18:9; Col 3:23; 2 Thess 3:10; 1 Tim 5:18), and he rewards labor (1 Tim 5:18). The members of a community marked by the kingdom of God have opportunities to engage in meaningful, materially rewarding work. Artists benefit from their activities when people pay for performances or objects. Artistic communication can also aid commerce in advertising. It can motivate and coordinate laborers. A thriving community values and rewards artists' contributions to its material health.

Category of Kingdom Goals: Scripture

Translating Scripture
Where the kingdom of God thrives, communities translate Scripture.

A community that demonstrates characteristics of God's kingdom has people who know what God has communicated through Scripture. Community members must first have access to a translation of the Bible that is faithful to the original documents. Their translation must communicate in ways that are clear to the majority of the community. It must deliver texts in the most appropriate and penetrating forms of the local language. Also, various Christian traditions must be able to use the translation. It must be easily transformed into oral communication forms. The Bible is filled with artistic forms of communication—parables, proverbs, stories, song lyrics, poetry. Insights into local artistic genres will likely help a community translate Scripture in ways that support Scripture translation goals.

Oral Scripture/Storytelling
Where the kingdom of God thrives, communities access Scripture through familiar forms.

A community marked by the kingdom of God has access to Scripture in many forms. Local art forms—especially those related to storytelling—can play key roles in integrating Scripture into community life.

Category of Kingdom Goals: Church Life

Corporate Worship
Where the kingdom of God thrives, Christ-followers gather to worship in ways that promote deep communication with God and each other.

Biblical worship is a life completely offered to God (Rom 12:1-2). It is the choice to live every moment for God's glory and not for one's own honor. Living a life of worship includes specific times of gathering with other believers for heartfelt adoration of God and communication with him (Ps 95:6; 96:9; Acts 2:42; Heb 10:24-25; Rev 19:10). Local arts provide languages for these moments of worshiping God and listening to him. The arts increase the use of our whole heart, soul, strength, and mind (Ps 100:2; Mark 12:29-30). Jesus taught that it doesn't matter where we worship, as long as we worship in spirit and in truth (John 4:21-24). Jesus's teaching opens the door for people from every nation and language to use their own forms of communication to worship and honor God.

Studying and Remembering Scripture
Where the kingdom of God thrives, communities understand and remember Scripture.

In a community that demonstrates more and more characteristics of God's kingdom, people study, remember, and understand Scripture. Studies show that memorizing words through song or motions involves more areas of the brain. Therefore, the more ways we learn Scripture—including through local arts—the more likely we are to remember it.

Christian Rites
Where the kingdom of God is strong, people mark important moments with intense spiritual events.

Important moments could include weddings, the Eucharist, funerals, rites of passage, and agricultural feasts. Artistic forms of communication indicate that certain events are special. Artistic expressions provide historical continuity through unique selections and forms. They open holistic channels of communication with God.

Witness
Where the kingdom of God thrives, non-believers learn about God.

In a community that demonstrates characteristics of God's kingdom, people learn that he is their Creator and Savior. Local arts are often intertwined with both special and daily activities of life. They signify important life events. They fill needs for social interaction and entertainment. Teaching includes local arts. Because daily life and local artistic expression are so interconnected, artistic communication provides a powerful way to communicate truth about God.

Category of Kingdom Goals: Personal Spiritual Life

Spiritual Formation
Where the kingdom of God thrives, Christ-followers experience spiritual growth.

Where the kingdom of God is strong, Christ-followers grow in their knowledge and experience of God, in their obedience to God, and in godly character traits and habits. Artistic forms of communication can energize and provide structure for formal and informal spiritual training, coaching, and mentoring.

Prayer and Meditation
Where the kingdom of God thrives, individuals have vibrant prayer lives.

A community that demonstrates characteristics of God's kingdom includes Christ-followers who communicate with God frequently and wholeheartedly. Because it's enjoyable, artistic expression can enhance this communication. It also connects deeply to people's emotions and wills.

Personal Bible Study
Where the kingdom of God thrives, individuals examine Scripture accurately and faithfully.

A community that demonstrates characteristics of God's kingdom has community members who examine Scripture accurately and faithfully. They integrate artistic forms of communication into their personal Bible study. Then they remember more, understand more, and are transformed more.

Applying Scripture
Where the kingdom of God thrives, communities apply the Bible to their lives.

In a community that demonstrates more and more characteristics of God's kingdom, people apply the teachings of Scripture to their daily life experiences. The Bible was written to people in different cultures and at different times. How can we accurately apply it to our lives today, in all different cultures? Local artistic communication helps people connect scriptural truths to their lives in memorable, motivating ways.

Unless you are working with Christians, the community you're with will not be motivated to work toward objectives stated as God's kingdom goals. Yet, because all humans are created in God's image, we all yearn for peace, health, joy, significance, and justice. You may call these attributes "Signs of a Better Future." When a community wants these things, we can wholeheartedly help its members, according to our skills and calling. If we are working with a local church, the goals will naturally include a deepening relationship to God. The ultimate King of the kingdom of God is Jesus. As we walk together with individuals and communities who don't know Jesus, our love and words can lead them to him.

Steps to Specifying Kingdom Goals

Having a list of kingdom goals and knowing which ones to pursue are two different things. Work with the community to determine which goals are important to them. Find out which goals they would like to accomplish. Creating together includes a continual process of identifying and modifying community goals. Follow the steps here to begin the process.

Talk with and listen to people.
Social structures (such as government organizations, churches, mosques, savings and credit associations, or conferences) provide a good place for conversation. You may want to gather a small group of people that represent different parts of the community to complete this activity.

Step 2

Explore & identify the strengths and aspirations of the community.

Ask people in the community what they have been doing well and what their hopes are for their children, themselves, and their community. The chart of strengths and aspirations identifies the presence of particular signs of the kingdom, at least as a hope.

Relate each strength or aspiration to a kingdom goal.

Put it in a chart for easy reference, such as the chart below (these are just examples).

Strengths and Aspirations	Related to these Kingdom Goals
Respect between generations	Identity and Sustainability
Celebration	Identity and Sustainability
Hospitality	Shalom

Explore the problems of the community.

Ask about issues that are difficult. Find out what causes significant worry. Ask what is worse in the community now compared to five, ten, or twenty years ago. Chart these in a similar fashion (see below) so that you can more easily see how they relate to kingdom goals. The chart of problems identifies the absence of particular signs of the kingdom.

Problems	Related to these Kingdom Goals
Disease: HIV/AIDS, malaria	Shalom
War, crime, violence	Shalom
Intergenerational conflict, loss of traditions	Identity and Sustainability
Fear of death	Personal Spiritual Life
Exploitation: slavery, prostitution	Justice
Inability to read or write	Justice
Lack of access to the Bible	Scripture
Lack of spiritual growth	Personal Spiritual Life
Lack of unity in Christian community	Church Life
Some groups left out of worship	Church Life
Inadequate communion with God	Personal Spiritual Life
Poor education	Justice
Hunger	Justice

Choose a goal.

Discuss which problem the community would most like to address. Talk about the strength they would most like to build on.

Write your results for Step 2 clearly.
State the chosen goal in the following format, filling in the community and goal below.

_____
COMMUNITY

has chosen

_____.
KINGDOM GOAL.

STEP 3

CONNECT GENRES TO GOALS

When community members have identified their community's goals, the next step is planning how their arts can help them reach those goals. Each artistic genre is particularly useful for communicating certain kinds of content. Each genre also produces certain effects. This section contains steps in the process of selecting genres and connecting them to kingdom goals.

Feasibility: Do resources exist that allow enactment of the genre? For example, are there people who know how to do this?

Events: Will an enactment of this genre help people think, feel, and act in ways that move them toward the kingdom goal? In what event?

Content: What content will contribute to the desired effects? Will connotations overpower or dilute the desired effects?

Choose the Desired Effects of the New Artistry

What effect do you want the arts to produce in the community? Some examples might be that community members understand an important message; act differently; change an unhelpful or dangerous behavior; do something new; think differently; feel solidarity with others; or experience hope, joy, anger, remorse, elation, peace, satisfaction, relief, empathy, surprise, or other emotions.

 Explore together how you want people to change in ways that move them toward kingdom goals. Write down the results of your discussion.

Choose the Content of the New Artistry

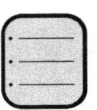 If the desired effects depend on people learning ideas through arts, make sure that the ideas are trustworthy.

Study the content to be taught so that an accurate message is conveyed. If the message is about how malaria may be prevented, make sure you know the facts. Talk to a health care professional. For Scripture, study the passage before creating a message based upon the passage. Talk to Bible scholars and translators. Talk about the content with God, other artists, and leaders.

Together, discuss and write down the answer to these questions:

- What content do we want to communicate?
- How can we make sure that the content is reliable?

Choose a Genre to Communicate the Content and Produce the Desired Effects

Every artistic genre has characteristics that affect the messages it conveys and the effects it has. Together, review the list of artistic genres you produced in Step 1. Review the Genre Comparison Chart you made, adding to it as necessary.

Genre	Brief Description	Event	Participants	Connotations	Effects	Institutions

Figure 8. Simplified Overview of Connecting Genre to Goals

For each genre, ask:

- Would a new artistic work in this genre have the effects we've chosen?
- If not, why not?
- Would a new artistic work in this genre effectively/accurately communicate the content we've chosen?
- If not, why not?

Narrow the list to one or two genres that would be the best for effecting these changes and communicating this content now.

Remember that all artistic genres have characteristics that can be redeemed for God's purposes. However, not all are appropriate at a given moment in a community's life. Encourage all involved to pray and listen for the wisdom of the Holy Spirit. Do not force a genre into new uses in a community unless the leaders involved deem it wise. Be certain that God wants it to happen now.

Step 3

Brainstorm about Events That Could Include a Performance of the New Work

 Before we start planning how to create new works in a genre, imagine the contexts for their presentation.

Think about how well the new works function as communication. Some examples of such communication contexts are listed in the chart below. Together, do the following:

- Make a list of events that new works in the artistic genre could be part of.
- Remind yourselves of your choices thus far: effects, content (messages), and genre.
- Choose a few of the event types you came up with and briefly describe them in terms of their communication components:
    - Who are the communicators?
    - When and where might such an event happen?
    - Which senses will participants use?
    - How will the genre affect the messages that people experience?
    - When people experience the artistry, will it have the effects you'd like?
    - How will people respond to the original communicators?
- Choose an event in which you might want to perform or present the new work.

Write your results for Step 3 in this form:

_____ will prepare
COMMUNITY

_____ that includes enactment of
EVENT

_____ with
GENRE(S)

_____ to produce
CONTENT

_____ that help
EFFECTS ON PEOPLE

_____ move toward
COMMUNITY

_____ .
KINGDOM GOAL

STEP 4

ANALYZE GENRES AND EVENTS

In order to create a new, effective piece, we must understand the genre it comes from. Step 4 suggests ideas for detailed analysis and exploration of the genre. As you learn more about art forms, remember that they change over time. Hold your descriptions lightly—things may be different tomorrow. Step 4 contains these components:[9]

- Choose an Artistic Event to Analyze
- Take a First Glance at an Event as a Whole
- Take a First Glance at an Event's Genre(s)
- Deepen Your Understanding of an Event's Forms by Looking Through Seven Lenses
- Relate the Event's Genre(s) to Its Broader Cultural Context
- Explore a Church's Arts

As you work through Step 4, you'll realize that not every research activity we include is relevant to the artistry you're investigating. Even if it were, you don't have enough time to do it all. Always do anything that starts with "Take a First Glance …" These provide a lot of insight requiring only a relatively small amount of energy and time. Then choose what else seems most pertinent or interesting. You'll be able to do enough.

---

[9] In the 2013 *CLAT Manual*, **Step 4** is divided into four sub-steps. We have not followed this organization in the *Abridged CLAT Manual*. Instead, we include the most helpful and accessible elements from **4A**, **4C**, and **4D**, leaving **4B**—research into complex artistic features—for more detailed form analyses.

> **SIMPLE ADVICE FOR AUDIO AND VISUAL RECORDING**
>
> Making recordings of artistic activities and products augments your memory. This allows you to review what happened, notice things you originally missed, repeatedly listen to or watch someone dancing to help you learn, and many other benefits. Here are a few basic ideas to help you make recordings more useful.
>
> Get the best recording equipment you can. Technology keeps changing, so it's impossible to tell you what particular equipment you should acquire. Ask other people where you live for advice, and learn how to use what you get.
>
> A bad recording is better than no recording at all. You should look for ways to increase your recording skills. But never let lack of experience keep you from recording something.
>
> Take back-up equipment with you. Equipment breaks when you least expect it. Take extra batteries, and any other recording devices you can.
>
> Make sure the kind of recording you're doing will fulfill your purposes. If you're planning to submit your recording to an archive or a media producer, you'll need to find out about their standards.
>
> Always get permission from everyone you're recording. Tell them how you plan to use the recordings, then ask them to agree or disagree. They can write it, or you can record them saying it.
>
> Document everything you record. Your recording will become worthless if you become unavailable some day and nobody knows what's on your recording. Therefore, write down what you record in a notebook, describing when, where, what, and whom you recorded. You can also record yourself saying, "This is [your name], recording [so-and-so person], at [such-and-such place], on [such-and-such day]."

Figure 9. Advice for Audio and Visual Recording

Choose an Artistic Event to Analyze

First, you need to decide which artistic event you want to learn more about. It's very important that you draw on actual experience to understand more about a community's arts. If all you do is talk with somebody in the abstract, you won't be able to trust your conclusions.

You may explore anywhere from one to hundreds of events—each will make your understanding of a genre richer. Refer to these guidelines that will help you choose an event to study.

> **CHARACTERISTICS OF AN ARTISTIC EVENT SUITABLE FOR STUDY**
>
> **Direct experience.** You need to be able to witness the event or objects firsthand, or have a good video recording of the event.
>
> **Chosen genre.** The event needs to contain an example of the genre the community has chosen to work with.
>
> **Community event.** The event must be done by people in the community.
>
> **Good example.** It will help if the event is typical of its genre and performed by artists the community states are skillful.

Figure 10. Characteristics of an Artistic Event Suitable for Study

Step 4

Take a First Glance at an Event as a Whole

Use the categories here to capture your preliminary observations, brief interviews, and assessments of an artistic event. You will explore each category in more detail later.

Context

Name of community: _____

Location (country, region, city/village, place): _____

_____

Date(s): _____

Your name: _____

The following categories relate fundamentally to forms of artistic communication.

SPACE
Was the event inside or outside?
Where were people placed in the location?
Did use of space change at different times? If so, how?

MATERIALS
What clothes, costumes, musical instruments, electronic media, amplification, and lighting did you notice?
Take photos and draw sketches if possible and desirable.

PARTICIPANT ORGANIZATION
Who was there?
How many people of each gender and age group were there?
Other demographic variables—Social status?
What were they doing?
How were they interacting?
Who organized, advertised, and promoted the event?

SHAPE OF THE EVENT THROUGH TIME
How long did the event last?
When did the event occur?
What were the major internal sections of the event itself?

PERFORMANCE FEATURES
What was everybody doing?
What activities were associated with this event, including pre- and post-event activities?

CONTENT
What kinds of plot, text, morals, themes, and language(s) were used?

UNDERLYING SYMBOLIC SYSTEMS
What meanings may be associated with the elements above?

The following categories relate fundamentally to how arts fit into a culture.

Apparent Purpose(s)

What was the occasion for the event?

Did people have a name for the event?

What were the people trying to achieve or accomplish in this event?

How were they trying to achieve it?

Were there any secondary goals that were either explicitly stated or tacitly understood?

How did the goals affect the event itself?

Emotions

How did the participants feel about the event?

How did others feel about the event?

What feelings were expressed through the event or in individual parts of the event, like a speech or song?

Community Values Shown

Did you see signs of hierarchical vs. egalitarian social structure, free vs. rigid atmosphere, conformity vs. nonconformity?

Were there clues in texts, spatial relationships, or interactions between participants?

Communal Investment

How many and what kinds of resources did the community invest in this event?

(This could include time in preparation, finances, length of performance, number of people involved, and status markers.)

Take a First Glance at an Event's Genre(s)

These simple questions help you focus on the type of artistry used in an event. There may be more than one type of artistic genre in an event, but apply these questions to only one at a time:

- What artistry do people produce (e.g., name of genre; kinds of activities like painting, acting, singing, dancing)?
- Who normally performs or creates it (e.g., women, men, children, caste members)? Also, gather names of prominent performers or creators.
- Where do people normally perform or create it (e.g., outdoors, indoors, special place)?
- When do people normally create or perform it (e.g., day night, ceremony, weekly rehearsal, spontaneously for pleasure)?
- To whom do people normally perform or present it (e.g., potential suitors, ecstatic audience, God)?
- Why do people normally perform or present it (e.g., to express emotions, make money, motivate to action, affirm identity, play)?
- With what connotations do people normally perform or present it (e.g., partying, a certain age group, spiritual, sexual)?
- How are new instances normally created (e.g., solitary individual, dreams, group experimentation)?

Step 4

Deepen Your Understanding of an Event's Forms by Looking through Seven Lenses

In physical terms, a lens is a special piece of glass. The glass is polished or otherwise changed to alter light coming through it. Depending on its maker's goal, a lens may make an object look closer, farther, or more deeply colored. A lens, then, is a way of bringing one aspect of an object into focus. We are using this same idea metaphorically to guide our research in the arts. In particular, we present a method that will guide your eyes, ears, nose, skin, and bodies to reveal seven categories of detail. The seven categories are space, materials, participant organization, shape of the event through time, performance features, content, and underlying symbolic systems.

Note that each of these lenses may interact very closely with the others. Some may describe the same thing from a different perspective. So don't be surprised if you come up with recurring patterns. Also, each lens may not reveal insights equally well in any given event. If one lens does not seem to help much, choose another through which to view the art.

We've designed these lenses to help you understand more about a particular event that has artistic content. If an event is the first you have seen of its type, you won't know yet what is normal. You also won't know what differs in significant ways from what usually happens. As you use the lenses to describe more events of this same type, you'll see both common patterns and differences.

LENS #1: SPACE

Space is the location, boundary markers, and physical characteristics of the area used for artistic communication. Space affects participants' movements and their relationships to one another. It lengthens or shortens the time participants need to move around in it. It also affects other elements of a performance.

Space is significant especially in events with dramatic and dance features. In addition, creators of artistic objects manipulate space. They create formal structure through features like proportion, rhythm, and balance.

 **To find out about space, perform activities like these:**

- Ask questions: Did it occur inside, outside, or both? What are some characteristics of the place where it happened (shape and size, for example)? What parts were the space separated into? What activities were associated with each part?
- Draw a floor diagram, including boundaries and demarcations.
- Take photographs of the place and its surroundings.
- Ask questions of participants and other cultural insiders about what happened. You may want to do this while watching a video of the event.
- Make a list of local names for the elements of space used in the event.

LENS #2: MATERIALS

Materials are all of the tangible things associated with an event. Clothing, regalia, instruments, props, and lighting are all materials. Some objects are more important to the execution and experience of the event than others. They may be made by humans (as in a mask) or designated to fill a function (as in an eagle feather marking regalia as royal). Objects may serve multiple purposes and convey meaning at many levels. For example, the Atumpan drum (Ghana) serves as a functional member of the musical ensemble. It also indicates royalty by its shape, colors, and construction. Therefore, it plays both a functional and symbolic role. Note also that some objects may not be a part of the event's activity.

Drama uses costumes and props to show characterization and provide dramatic settings. The most common objects used to produce musical features are instruments. In dance, costumes and props may highlight motion. A storyteller might use a prop to symbolize an event in her story. Visual artists use all sorts of materials to create objects.

To find out about materials, perform activities like these:

Make a list of objects associated with the event, by asking questions:
- What objects were present, including structures (like buildings)?
- What objects did people bring expressly for the event?
- What did people wear?
- What did people hold, kick, or otherwise manipulate with their bodies?
- Were there foods or drinks involved in the event?

For each object, write down this information:
- What are local and other names for the object?
- What are the object's physical characteristics? (This may include materials, design, construction, weight, and length. Kinds of source materials include fibers [from plants or animals], minerals, metals, plastics, and wood.)

LENS #3: PARTICIPANT ORGANIZATION

At an artistic event, virtually everyone present participates in some way (and sometimes people who aren't even there participated by way of preparation). Each participant in an event plays a role that affects the form of the performance. Roles can include creators, performers (e.g., singers, instrument players, actors, dancers, storytellers); audience (e.g., aficionados, spectators, hecklers); helpers (e.g., set builders, stage managers, gaffers, ticket takers, bouncers, ushers); producers, directors, and others. Participants' histories are also relevant to the formal characteristics of an event. A participant's history may include their skills, kin and other relationships, status and role in everyday life, and ethnic, religious, and social identities. For example, a priest may be the only one who can play certain roles in a religious ceremony.

Step 4

 **To find out about participants, perform activities like these:**
- Ask questions:
  - How many participants were there (be sure to include ancestors or gods that are not physically present)?
  - What were each of their roles?
  - How did the participants use performance features to interact with each other?
  - Were there obvious patterns (etiquette)?
  - Are there local names for the participant roles used in the event?
  - What are salient characteristics of each participant, in terms of training, ability, reputation, and professional/caste status?
- Make audio, video, and photographic documentation of the event.
  - Ask a friend involved in the event what role(s) you might be able to fill in this type of event. Note what background and competencies you would have to have or acquire to fill different roles. When appropriate and possible, prepare to perform a role for a future event of this type.
- Make a timeline, noting participants' actions and interactions.
- Ask questions of participants and other cultural insiders about what happened. You may want to do this while watching a video of the event.

As usual, look for meaning, symbolism, and broader cultural themes.

LENS #4: SHAPE OF THE EVENT THROUGH TIME

One way to describe the shape of an event is by dividing it into chronological parts. Identify the time that one segment ends and the next begins by noting significant changes in elements of the event. Notice the changes when you view them through each of the other lenses. These changes are called markers. For example, markers could include pauses or sudden contrasts in participants' features. They could involve the beginning and ending of participants' activities or the beginning and ending of songs.

An example from a genre with many dramatic features is a play, broken into acts and scenes, and then into gestures and movements. A concert could be described hierarchically as consisting of songs, verses, phrases, and notes. Dance genres may consist of pieces, motifs, and gestures. An oral verbal art like a poem may contain stanzas, lines, and beats.

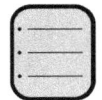 **To find out about the shape of an event, perform activities like these:**
- Make audio and video recordings of the event.
  - Create a Hierarchical Segmentation Timeline, following these steps:

Step One

While watching or listening to the recording, make a timeline of the event, noting what happens at different times.

Time	What Happened
13:30	Storytellers began to arrive
...	...
...	...
14:27	Everyone left the area

Step Two

Watch or listen to the recording again, noting what seem to be important transition points (you may need to do this with somebody who has been part of such an artistic event). Then make a chart with the largest segments along the top. You may continue dividing subsegments at finer timescales, down to the level of your research interest.

Segment 1 (5 min.)		Segment 2 (12 min.)			Segment 3 (10 min.)		Segment 4 (3 min.)		
1A	1B	2A	2B	2C	3A	3B	4A	4B	4C

LENS #5: PERFORMANCE FEATURES

Performance features are the results of what people do in an event, the characteristics of a performance. A performer uses unique skills and processes during an event. He or she knows the essential rules of the artistic form. A performer must master the rules to make the event successful. Categories of performance features are listed below.

Step 4

CATEGORIES OF PERFORMANCE FEATURES

Vocal features: Participants use vocal features in drama to help them act. Vocal features in music help participants sing. In dance, vocal manipulation helps participants coordinate breath with movement patterns. In oral verbal arts, vocal modification creates effects by changing the pitch or timbre of the performers' voices.

Body movements: In dramatic performances, participants use body movements in acting, characterization, and space organization. In music, participants use their bodies to play instruments. In dance, phrasing and body and space organization involve body movements. In oral verbal arts, participants use their bodies to gesture.

Object manipulation: In drama, people manipulate objects to help them act. In music, object manipulation helps performers play instruments and modify their voices. In dance, people manipulate objects to support movement. In oral verbal arts, object manipulation emphasizes speech elements. In visual arts, participants make or present a communicative object.

Visual characteristics: Visual features play important roles in dramatic events and dance. Visual roles include costumes, makeup, puppets, and other elements. In visual arts, design and composition incorporate visual features.

Rhythm: Rhythmic features that contribute to musical characteristics include polyrhythm, proportional rhythm, and free rhythm. Polyrhythm is contrasting rhythms played simultaneously. Proportional rhythm is smaller rhythmic units that are proportions of larger units. Free rhythm is a rhythm with no clear pattern.

Narration: Narrating features play significant roles in presenting or recounting events in drama and oral verbal arts.

Poetic devices: Finally, participants may use poetic devices for acting in drama, in song lyrics, and throughout oral verbal arts.

Figure 11. Categories of Performance Features

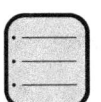

To find out about an event's performance features, perform activities like these:

While experiencing an event (either live or recorded), write a free-flowing account of your answers to these questions:

- What sounds did you hear?
- What movements, colors, lights, and shapes did you see?
- What aromas did you smell? What sensations did you feel?
- What flavors did you taste?

While observing an event (either live or recorded), write a free-flowing account of your answers to these questions:

- What did participants do with their voices?
  Common vocal actions include singing, acting, orating, narrating, or producing sound effects.
- What did participants do with their bodies?
  Common bodily actions include acting, instrument playing, and dancing.
- What did participants do with their words?

Common word-related activities include poetry, singing, acting, orating, and narrating.

- What did participants do with objects?
Common actions with objects include instrument playing, acting, creating spectacle, dancing, oratory, narrating, and presenting a communicative object.

LENS #6: CONTENT

Content refers to the subject matter or topics of an artistic event. It is most closely tied to symbols like words and movements in signed languages or dances. Multiple layers of meanings may exist, and meaning may be implied or explicit. To understand content, you have to connect to people who know the language and other communication systems really well … don't just guess.

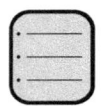

To find out about an event's content, perform activities like these:

- Record the event. Ask a friend to write down important words that people uttered and meanings of any symbolic motions that occurred.
- Ask participants what they intended to communicate during the event.
- Ask participants what emotions or actions they hoped to elicit in other people because of the event.
- Ask participants what topics were angering, humorous, boring, or rousing to them.

LENS #7: UNDERLYING SYMBOLIC SYSTEMS

An event's participants share a common mental and emotional background. During a performance, they use shared rules, expectations, grammatical structures, motivations, and experiences to decide what to do at any given moment. Their shared knowledge and understanding are underlying symbolic systems. Underlying symbolic systems inform composition and interpretation.

Some underlying systems are simple and easy to find. For example, Indonesian gamelan has a cyclic pattern. The pattern is quickly discernible by noticing that the ensemble's big gong sounds at regular intervals. Similarly, a Strauss waltz divides metrically into groups of three beats. The first beat is always accented, so the Strauss waltz does not require extensive analysis. As another example, audiences can quickly identify Thai likay drama's stock characters after hearing a brief description of the characters' behavior and costume conventions.

Understanding other underlying systems may be more difficult. You may need to do intensive analysis using rigorous methodology. You may need to interview participants and even participate yourself. For example, grammatical rules governing melodic or rhythmic structure of a song are not always obvious. The allowable movements in a dance may not be apparent. Details of an artist's use of space in a painting are often not immediately evident.

Detailed discovery of underlying symbolic systems is beyond the scope of this manual.

Step 4

Relate the Event's Genre(s) to its Broader Cultural Context

Artistry is always intertwined with other realities in communities. You will only fully understand the musical, dramatic, dance, verbal, visual, or culinary features of artistry with a more complete picture of the community.

To help you gain more insight into how an art form fits into its culture, investigate the areas below. Again, choose activities that seem most relevant and interesting.

Artists

Any plan a community makes to draw on its arts for kingdom goals must have the understanding of, and interaction with, artists at its core. They are the ones God is calling us to learn from, welcome, and encourage. They are the central actors in our co-creation activities.

To find out about a genre's artists, perform activities like these:

Get to know the artists involved in the art form you are studying. You may decide to study formally or informally with a skilled artist. Join artists in their personal and artistic worlds. Sit with a composer and see how he or she creates. Ask to watch an artist teach someone else. Share your own life and artistic gifts with him or her.

Ask questions:
- How do artists in this genre relate to their community?
- What status does an artist hold in the community?
- Is there a difference in the status based on the type of art they do (such as drumming for royalty, creating songs for important events in a person's life, lewd drama for a brothel, etc.)?
- How do people become artists in this genre?
- Is it based on societal patterns (artist caste), achieved by individual effort and skill, or a combination?

Creativity

Every community makes things that never existed before. But each community—and each artistic genre—thinks about and creates new things in different ways.

To find out about a genre's approach to creativity, perform activities like these:

Observe, participate in, and commission new works. As you participate in the creative process, you can discover how new works are created and who creates them.

Ask questions:
- Are new works created deliberately and consciously, or received through visions?
- Are new works created by an individual or a group?
- What techniques are used to create (improvisation, community creation, individual crafting)?
- Does the community value more highly work that departs from tradition or work that enhances tradition?

Language

The language, or languages, and types of language an artistic event uses can reveal much about the event's relationship to its broader cultural context. Song lyrics in a regional or national language support regional or national identity. A tapestry woven with a minority language's unique alphabet may accentuate identification with a minority community. Archaic or special words not used in everyday speech are also common in artistic communication. Using archaic language may reflect a sense of mystery or fear associated with the genre. The genre may also be preserved in ancient form for other reasons.

To find out about a genre's use of language, perform activities like these:

Watch or listen to a recording of an event, or look at an object with someone who knows a lot about it. List every component containing language, and write down answers to questions like these:

- What language or dialect is this in? Are there some words in other languages?
- Can you imagine someone saying this in normal speech, or is it a special kind of language?

Transmission and change

An important theme throughout this manual is that everything changes over time. People pass on their skills and knowledge to other people, but this transmission never happens perfectly. Transmission may happen through formal training, informal observation, mentoring, or individual exploration.

To find out about how a genre has changed in its history and how it is changing now, perform activities like these:

- Ask participants in the event you are examining to tell how they learned to do what they did. Ask if you can participate in or watch that process sometime. As you watch, note the interactions between people, how more knowledgeable people are treated, and what objects are part of the process.
- If this event is part of a long tradition, ask an older person how and when people used to learn it. Then ask if they still learn it this way, and if not, what has changed to make the difference.
- Find old and newer recordings or examples of an art form. Watch or listen to them with a knowledgeable person, and ask how the two differ. Ask what might have caused differences.

Cultural dynamism

Healthy communities maintain a mix of continuity and change. Artistic genres support community vitality through interactions between the genre's stable and malleable elements. A genre's stable elements are components that do not change. They occur regularly in time and place. Stable elements are tightly organized. A genre's malleable elements change with time. They are less predictable (perhaps marked by improvisation) and more loosely organized. Cultural dynamism happens when artists masterfully use their arts' most malleable elements to strengthen the most stable elements.

 **To find out about how dynamic a genre is, and how its dynamism is produced, ask participants in an event questions like these:**

- To identify stable artistic elements: Which art forms or aspects of art forms occur most regularly, with tight organization and the least amount of variability?
- To identify malleable artistic elements: Which art forms or aspects of art forms occur with less predictability and are more loosely organized?
- To identify interactions between stable and malleable elements: How do these stable and malleable aspects interact?

Identity and power

Communities can use artistic performance to affirm or oppose social status and authority. Sometimes particular art forms allow people with less status to communicate openly about their problems with others. Misunderstanding how people view power relationships can lead to unnecessary controversy.

 **To find out about how identity and power are reflected in an event, perform activities like these:**

- Transcribe any texts associated with this event, like song lyrics or story content. Examine them to see if there are overt messages affirming or opposing a person, institution, or other entity. Discreet discussion with a friend may help you find out if there are any hidden messages.
- Observe the event. Did people communicate messages in the event that challenged authority in ways you haven't seen them do elsewhere? Artistic action can provide a safe place for contestation or resolving conflict.
- Ask participants in an event questions like these: How is authority affirmed or opposed in the artistic expression? Who is participating in the art and why? Do hidden messages exist? Do overtly communicated messages affirm or oppose a person or institution?

Aesthetics and evaluation

Humans quickly judge others' arts by their own artistic standard. We must help ourselves and others not do this. You can find out how people in the community you're working with approach correction and evaluation in general.

To find out about aesthetics and evaluation, perform activities like these:

- Ask a friend how (or if) he or she would correct someone older or younger. Ask how (or if) he or she would correct someone in roles of higher or lower status. Members of the community might value direct correction in some contexts. They might require indirect correction in other situations.
- Ask the same friend how the kinds of people he or she just described would correct him or her.

Learn more about evaluation of an artistic object's form by doing the following:

- Ask people what makes a component of the form good or bad.
- Observe experts teaching the form to someone else—perhaps you. Write down what advice the experts give. Write down mistakes they correct. You may see the ideal form by listening to the advice given and the mistakes made.
- Notice items that are put in a place of prominence. Pay attention to items people speak about with respect. Observe items people need special expertise and time to create. Prominent, respected, and special creations likely have ideal characteristics. Ask people what makes them good or pleasing.

Time

People often think about and experience time in particular ways in an event. Participants may feel time passing more quickly, more slowly, or in unpredictably complex ways. In addition, the structure, flow, and timing of a performance may intersect with broader cultural temporal patterns. Finally, in many communities, certain events only occur at particular points in agricultural, religious, or other calendrical cycles.

To find out about time in an event, perform activities like these:

- Soon after an event, ask participants questions like these: How did you know when to do certain things? How did you experience time? Did it feel like things happened one after another, in repeating cycles, or flowing in waves? Did it feel sacred? When else do you experience time this way?
- Ask experts in a genre to describe the passage of time during performance. Do they explicitly connect this description to broader calendrical cycles?

Step 4

Emotions

Capacity to express and evoke emotion is one of the most celebrated characteristics of artistic communication. The arts have a way of connecting a sound, sight, movement, scent, or taste directly to potent, emotionally charged memories. They also often provide a socially acceptable release for intense feelings, as lamentations and wailing do for grief.

To find out about emotions, perform activities like these:

- Watch a recording of an event and write down what emotions participants—including audience members—appear to express. Ask someone who was there if they agree with your interpretations.
- Watch a video recording of an artistic event with people who were there. Watch the observers, and when they exhibit any emotion—joy, surprise, sadness, anger, disdain, etc.—stop the recording and ask yourself about what they're responding to. Make a list of the words they use to describe their emotions and what was going on in the performance that sparked them.

Subject matter

Songs, proverbs, plays, tapestries, and other arts have verbal content. The content comes from the minds, experiences, and histories of the participating individuals and communities. Artistic communication sometimes uncovers information that is nearly inaccessible otherwise. Artists can sometimes convey ideas about topics that are usually unexpressed.

Other times artistic communication reveals the values of the community in memorable form. Proverbs are a strong example of values revealed memorably. References in textual content may be metaphorical or cryptic. Your first understanding may not be the only one.

To find out about subject matter, perform activities like these:

Make a list of the elements in an event that have verbal content, like songs, proverbs, or stories. Ask an expert to describe the messages in each. Ask:

- What is this about?
- What are they trying to communicate?
- Is there a lesson?
- If so, who is the lesson for?

As you watch a recording or read a transcription of an event, ask a small group of participants to list all of the references to people, objects, places, events, or spiritual beings. Ask them to describe each. Record or write down their answers.

Community values shown

Artistic communication often provides community members with a place to challenge community authorities. However, how artists organize and perform the communication may also reveal important aspects of a community's values and social structures. Reflect on the physical and social organization of participants to gain insight into broader community values.

 To explore relationships between an artistic event and broader community values, perform activities like these:

Observe an event, then ask questions:

- How do participants interact with representatives of authority within the event?
- How does this differ from such interactions in other contexts?
- Does the physical organization of participants show a hierarchical structure, as in the first, second, and third seats of performers in the sections of a symphony orchestra, or are participants organized on the same physical level?

Answers to these questions may reflect values of hierarchical vs. egalitarian social structures elsewhere in the community.

- In what ways, if any, are participants encouraged to express themselves individually? What signs of free vs. rigid atmosphere are there?

Answers to these questions may reflect values of conformity vs. non-conformity elsewhere in the community.

Communal investment

The amount of energy that members of a community invest in different kinds of artistic activity varies widely. A grandfather speaking a proverb to his granddaughter involves only two people. It requires no preparation, costs no money, and lasts for only a few seconds. A funeral for a king in western Cameroon, on the other hand, may last a month. It may include hundreds of people. It may also require significant finances to pay for food, transportation, and gifts.

 To find out about a community's investment in an event, observe, ask, and write down information about the following:

- length of time of performance
- status of scheduling: high status time, low status time
- amount of preparation
- cost of the performance
- location of the performance: high status, low status
- performance space: status, size, expense, exclusivity
- participants: number, status, exclusivity, level of skill or professionalism
- complexity: number of relevant features

Step 4

Explore a Church's Arts

If there is a church in a community, we want to help it expand the kingdom of God inside and outside its walls. So we've developed tools that relate specifically to Christian communities. We treat churches as special communities for at least two reasons. First, the church is Christ's body (Col. 1:24), so we care very deeply about how those within a community church live. Second, churches exist in particular places, but they also connect with people in different places. These broader communities could include regional denominations, foreign mission organizations, Catholic or Orthodox orders, and others. So to help a church serve God more completely, we need to help them look at all of their arts, no matter where they come from.

To help you help churches, we've included two activities. The first one—Identify and Evaluate the Arts Used in a Church—consists of three sub-activities. The second activity—Compare Musical Instruments in the Old Testament—shows how the same instruments can be used for many different purposes.

Identify and Evaluate the Arts Used in a Church

1. Discover a Church's Arts

The approach to identifying a church's artistic life is similar to what we described for the broader community in "Take a First Glance at a Community's Arts" (Step 1). Put whatever you discover into the Community Arts Profile. Gather leaders and participants in various aspects of church life, and lead them through activities like these:

List all of the contexts in which people act as part of this church.

These contexts could include—but are not limited to—the following: Bible studies, home groups, Sunday school, adult education, corporate worship services, spiritual mentorships, Mass, Vacation Bible School, children's ministries, food pantry, visits to people who are sick, rites (like baptism, weddings, and funerals), healing services, holiday celebrations, social outings, retreats and camps, outreach activities, festivals, concerts, prayer vigils, and individual or family devotions. Use the table below to get started.

Church Events and Activities	Which (if any) Artistic Genres Used?

List any arts used in each of these contexts.

For each context the group has listed, write down whether people use any form of artistic communication (genres). If so, write what that form is.

Common kinds of arts in Christian communities include singing, preaching, drama, storytelling, sculpting, carving, designing space, incense, dancing, making banners, drawing, reading, or reciting poetry. Note also that rituals are common in Christian communities. They may be artistic events in themselves (e.g., as forms of drama or pageantry), and they often include artistic elements. Use the table above to get started.

List all of the people who have significant artistic gifts, whether they use them in the church or not.

For each person in the Christian community with artistic training and gifts, list the kind(s) of arts they have skills in and their particular competencies (e.g., composing, performing, drawing). Church leadership may be unaware of many of the gifts that its members have. In this case, you may want to help them perform a more thorough investigation through a simple questionnaire or oral investigation. Use the table below to get started.

People with Artistic Training or Gifts	Which Genre(s)?

2. Compare a Christian Community's Use of Arts to That of Its Surrounding Communities

These steps will help churches decide how to better connect to the people in their geographical context. See especially "Church Life" and "Personal Spiritual Life" in Step 2. Remember that this is part of a broader process in which churches critically evaluate different artistic genres for potential use. Use the table on the next page to get started.

- Consult the list you made on the previous page of all the kinds of arts that the Christian community uses in everything it does.

- Consult the list you created in Step 1 of artistic genres used in the church's surrounding community.

- Mark each genre of artistic communication that exists both in the church and in its surrounding community.

- For each genre that exists in both, discuss and write down ways in which their performance and purpose differ in each context.

- Make a list of all the genres in the surrounding community that are not used in the church. Discuss reasons why these are not being used, and explore their potential for use.

Step 4

Artistic Genres Used in the Church	Used Outside the Church? (Yes/No)

3. Evaluate How a Christian Community's Arts Currently Fulfill Its Purposes

In Step 2, we highlighted a few reasons that a Christian community might act to extend the kingdom of God: to deepen corporate worship, improve spiritual formation, extend its witness, etc. A brief survey of how people used the arts in the Bible reveals a longer list: celebrate victory (Ex.15), accompany processions (2 Sam. 6), adoration (2 Chron. 5), cultural festivals (2 Chron. 35:15), repentance (Psalm 51), dancing (1 Chron. 15), funerals (Matt. 9:23), strengthen the church (1 Cor. 14:26), express happiness (James 5:13), express sadness (Psalm 6), spiritual warfare (2 Chron. 20:21-23), and healing (1 Sam 16). It's important to remember that not every use of the arts shown in Scripture serves as a positive example—Aaron crafted a golden calf as an idol (Ex. 32), but we should not imitate him.

In addition, the Bible points to even more purposes of the church, including confession, witness, prayer, teaching, thanksgiving, discipleship, lamentation, evangelism, encouragement, exhortation, mind renewal, reconciliation, forgiveness, correction, commemoration, building solidarity, creating contextual equivalents, and testimony. Though we can't create an exhaustive list of all potential purposes, we do believe that it is essential that each church identify the reasons it does things, so it can evaluate whether the arts it uses helps achieve its goals. This process may also reveal additional biblical aims that the community should adopt. The following steps can help do this (use the tables below to get started):

- Consult the list of all the contexts in which people act as part of their Christian community.
- Choose one context in which artistic communication exists, and list its purposes. Refer to the paragraphs above for ideas.
- List ways in which the form(s) of artistic communication used in each context support or detract from its purposes. Discuss these and suggest changes the church could make.
- Use what you've discovered for sparking activities in Step 5.
- Repeat with other events and activities of the church.
- One event in which arts are used in the church: _____

Purpose(s) of the Event	Arts Used in the Event

Do the Arts Used in the Event Support or Detract from the Event's Purposes?

Compare Musical Instruments in the Old Testament

Sometimes churches develop negative associations with particular artistic objects (e.g., instruments) or genres. The chart below helps show how objects have no inherent moral value: instead, it is the heart of the person using an object that determines whether or not God is pleased with that object. Help a group discover this truth for themselves by starting with an empty chart and following these steps:

1. Write the Scripture references and version along the top of a chalkboard or whiteboard.

2. Ask someone to read each passage aloud; then ask the group to identify each instrument that was mentioned. Write the names of the instruments under the passage.

3. Ask the group to note instruments that occur in more than one column. Circle those.

4. Ask the group to describe the purpose of each event. Write this purpose under each passage.

5. Ask the group if they can find a correlation between certain instruments and certain purposes.

6. Ask what principles they can derive from this exercise. Then discuss how they can apply these principles to the use of arts in their church.

Daniel 3:5 king's court (false worship)	Isaiah 5:12 drunken party (secular)	Psalm 150 praising God (true worship)	2 Sam. 6:5; 1 Chron. 15:16–29 religious procession (true worship)
flute (end-blown)		flute (end-blown)	
animal horn trumpet		shofar trumpet	shofar trumpet silver trumpets
reed pipe	reed pipe		
lyre	lyre	lyre	lyre
larger lyre	larger lyre	larger lyre	larger lyre
bow harp		string and woodwind instruments	
all kinds of instruments			
	frame drum	frame drum	frame drum
		cymbals	cymbals
		loud cymbals	
			rattle

		dance	dance

STEP 5

SPARK CREATIVITY

A sparking activity is anything anybody does to create new artistry. In different places, acts of creativity will require different amounts of community investment, from low to high. For example, during an afternoon meeting, someone might suggest that a friend creates a painting in response to a speech. Her simple suggestion sparks the creation of a new painting. The suggestion involves low community investment. Planning a festival is a more complex act of creativity. It may include many artists and government officials. Planning a festival is an act of creativity that requires high community investment.

A sparking activity may lead to immediate reward. It might also provide a structure for future creativity to happen. For example, artists may learn how to make, tune, and play a traditional instrument through a sparking activity. Their learning lays the foundation for composing new songs in the future. Finally, sparking activities may apply many or all of the seven Creating Local Arts Together (CLAT) steps, or they may focus on just one of the steps. Workshops often include times to identify kingdom goals (Step 2), perform initial analysis of a genre (Step 4), and create and improve works (Step 5). Other activities may focus solely on creating. In any case, the community needs to see the sparking activity in the context of the whole co-creation process.

How to Organize a Sparking Activity

A. Prepare to draw on familiar methods of composition.

Each community, and especially each creative individual, has patterns to create art. You want to make use of their patterns as much as possible. In a Mono example (Democratic Republic of the Congo), someone asked a musician to compose a new example of gbaguru based on one of Jesus's parables. The musician asked questions, thought a while, and started playing a repeated pattern on his kundi. Then he said he needed to be by himself to compose the song. Other composers may work in a pair or group. Some composers may choose to use pencil and paper. Some receive inspiration in dreams or visions. Some composers work on paid commission. Others employ spontaneous improvisation. Composers may use any number of methods in creating new works. The activity you and the community design will likely include both familiar and new kinds of invention.

 **Describe how new examples of the genre you've chosen come about. How are they created?**

B. Think carefully about the key composer(s).

We use the word "composer" here to include anyone who creates something, including painters, weavers, dramatists, and the like. We cannot do without the key composer because of his or her artistic abilities, skill, and influence on others. Look for the person, or people, who will create the best works. The key composer should also have the social credentials to help the project spread in the community.

In some communities, many such qualified people may be available. In other places, the choices may be limited. Sometimes, for example, choosing certain genres will automatically determine the gender of the composer and performer. Local people will be able to make a list of potential experienced composers.

In some cultures, communities have an established role for composers who create songs for other people. In West Africa, especially in areas influenced by Islam, a local form of griot (praise singer) may be present. In examples from Nigeria, Benin, and Ghana, a Muslim praise singer agreed to work with a biblical text to compose and record a Scripture song.[10] Investigate the musical culture in your area. See if an established form of composing for patrons already exists. Such professional composers are used to working for a cash payment. "Composers-for-hire" also appear in some Asian cultures, including parts of Nepal and the Philippines.

If you work in a Christian community, finding someone who is both a Christian and an experienced composer may be difficult. In certain artistic genres, finding that kind of person may be almost impossible. In this case, consider commissioning the work from a non-Christian composer. You should ask the following questions:

- Is the composer interested?
- Is he or she respected by members of the community?
- If his or her name is made known, will that help or hinder acceptance of the work?
- What do local Christians think of the idea?

---

10 Klaus Wedekind, "The Praise Singers," *Bible Translator* 26, no. 2 (1975): 245–47.

Step 5

 **Discuss the kind of composer you would like to have, how available he or she is likely to be, particular people who might fill the role, and how best to interact with them.**

C. Identify opportunities to maximize and barriers to overcome.

In the community, identify barriers and opportunities associated with creativity in the genre. Here are a few common examples of each:

Opportunities
- talented artists eager to use their gifts in new contexts
- government interest in promoting local art forms
- growing recognition of the value of local arts and fear for their loss in the wider community
- a respected champion of local arts in the community; someone who can lead innovation

Barriers
- negative attitudes toward use of local language and art forms in some domains
- lack of knowledge and skills associated with a genre
- apathy toward change in the community
- weakening of interest in local cultural forms due to urbanization and globalization

 After discussing these examples with members of the community, ask:
- What might help us spark abundant development of new works in this genre?
- How could we draw on these opportunities when designing a sparking activity?
- What might stop us from achieving this development?
- How could we overcome these barriers when designing a sparking activity?

D. Organize an activity

There are many types of activities that spark creativity. Below are several types of activities that you could choose, depending on the need.

Commissioning

Ask an artist or group of artists to create a new instance of an artistic genre for an agreed-upon purpose. Commissioning commonly consists of these steps:

1. With the community, identify the event for which the item will be created:
   - the purpose(s) for the created item (e.g., literacy, church worship, community development);
   - the genre of creation (e.g., haiku, olonkho, Broadway musical);
   - the content; and
   - the creator(s).

2. Then,
   - work with the maker(s) in the creative process, including evaluation and revision of the work(s);
   - prepare the rest of the community and the event organizers for a public presentation;
   - explore other distribution means, including recordings; and
   - explore ways that this work, and others like it, can enter into other domains of the community's life.

Find out what sort of compensation is appropriate for the artist, genre, and event. Compensation may be in the form of money, services, goods, social capital, or goodwill borne of friendship. Develop respect and trust with the artist(s).

Think through the commissioner's roles during the composition process. Who will decide what is good and what needs to be changed? How much freedom will the artist have to innovate? As much as possible, the commissioner and artist should agree on their roles before the composition process begins.

You may also commission yourself to create a new work, but always commission yourself only in relationship with the community.

Workshops

Workshops are short events—typically one or two weeks—that gather people to make progress together on a particular task. When participants interact with each other in a concentrated way, a lot can be accomplished and produced.

Having an organization take care of a workshop's logistics is helpful. Setting goals for the workshop is also important. Goals may be composing songs for church worship or creating and recording works with dramatic content to be distributed through radio or other media. See the full Manual, Step 4D, for a sample workshop outline. See the Handbook DVD by Todd and Mary Beth Saurman for "Ideas for Arts Workshop Modules."

Showcase events

You may help a community plan or run a festival or competition that highlights creativity in local artistic genres. Festivals are events designed to showcase a community's cultural identity and creative output. Ethnic or religious groups that already have celebratory gatherings may be open to including new works of art produced by Christians. Starting a new festival tradition may also be possible. New traditions can be fueled by Christians' celebration of their God-given artistic gifts. Prizes for the best new works add energy and excitement. Festivals provide great opportunities for cooperation between different Christian, cultural, religious, and other groups within a community.

Showcase events normally have five stages:

1. **Imagining and planning:** How will we get from here to there? The larger the event, the more planning it requires. Some communities excel in creating detailed schedules and goals. Other communities excel in pulling together fabulous celebrations through organic social dynamics. Contribute ideas, but don't impose a system.

2. **Promotion and networking:** How can we ensure the participation of key artists and a wide public? Festivals sometimes incorporate contests or prizes to motivate artists. Make sure to clearly communicate the kinds of arts that will be rewarded and how they will be evaluated.
3. **Composition of and preparation for performance:** Will artists have time and resources to create and practice?
4. **Running the event itself:** Try to create a sense of common purpose, flexibility, and joy as the event unfolds. Also, try to get as many people as possible to play roles in making the event happen.
5. **Evaluation and planning:** Dedicate time after the event to graciously evaluate how it went with key people. See how the event relates to the seven CLAT steps. Discuss the possibility of similar future events.

Mentoring

Sometimes because of your age, education, or social position, you may enter a long-term relationship that benefits an individual artist or group of artists. This relationship usually develops over time from personal rapport and common goals. Mentors may help influence a mentee's professional, spiritual, and character growth. A mentoring relationship may open doors to new opportunities. It may also allow sharing instructive stories from each individual's own life. Mentorship includes reciprocal learning as well. If the relationship crosses cultures, the mentee will teach the mentor skills and cultural insights. Over time, the bond between mentor and mentee often grows increasingly deep and satisfying.

Structured apprenticeship

Apprenticeship provides a structure consistent with existing cultural forms. In an apprenticeship, artistic experts can transfer their skills and knowledge to other members of their community. Structured apprenticeship makes sense when experts in a genre exist, when contexts for transfer of competencies in the genre are declining, and when community members value the genre. A community may institute such a program in this way:

1. Choose the genre to be taught.
2. Choose a master of the genre.
3. Choose the apprentices.
4. Design a training context that
    a. draws on familiar educational forms;
    b. includes a place, time, and frequency that the master and apprentices can commit to;
    c. covers the knowledge, skills, and attitudes crucial to the genre; and
    d. lasts long enough for apprentices to reach a sustainable level of competency.
5. Implement the program.
6. During the program, explore how participants can continue to develop their skills and perform in various contexts

Publications

Almost any activity will have more long-term success if it turns thoughts and artistic production into recorded media. Paper, recordings, and electronic data of all kinds allow ideas and artistry to live beyond a single moment. Publications reach people beyond a single place. Periodicals and websites make it possible to disseminate information and inspire discussion on a wide range of topics. Audio and video products provide content for training programs and entertainment. Publications become repositories of history and biography when people begin to forget what came before them. General aspects to planning a publication include the following:

- Determine the target audience.
- Identify editors, advisors, and contributors.
- Solicit, select, and prepare the materials to be published.
- Determine a scheme for the distribution of the publication.
- Determine a schedule for ongoing publication.
- Carry out the publication and distribution.

Develop and use feedback tools (electronic comments, letters to the editor, surveys, etc.) to help determine past effectiveness and plan for future developments.

Creators' clubs

Artists often form associations, clubs, and fellowships to encourage each other, critique each others' work, share resources and ideas, perform, and collaborate on products. Artists' clubs meet regularly in certain places and times. They have expectations—however modest—of each other. They often focus on a particular art form and purpose.

Each group will look different, but you should consider the following ideas when starting or modifying a group:

- Choose a meeting place and time that accommodates the members and allows for artistic activity.
- Discuss the goals for the group and the expectations of its members. The objectives could vary from very fluid and informal to strict and explicit, depending on the group's wishes.
- If the group forms part of a church or wants to create things for Christian communities, integrate spiritual formation into its activities. Artists act like God in their creativity (except that he creates out of nothing). Sometimes, however, artists get drawn into unhealthy applications of the power they yield. Prayer, Bible study, accountability, and other disciplines provide a spiritual anchor for all artists' creative directions and performance.

Step 5

 **Discuss and choose the type of activity that would work best in this CLAT process.**

 **Describe the activity you will use**

Using Figure 12 as a guide, describe each element of the sparking activity the community has chosen to perform.

THINGS TO WRITE DOWN WHEN DESIGNING A SPARKING ACTIVITY

Title and summary: a brief overview of the activity and its main purposes. Include its overall type: commissioning, workshop, showcase event, mentoring, apprenticeship, publication, creators' club, or other. Overview should not be more than one paragraph long.

Participants: all of the types of people who need to be involved for the activity to succeed. This may include creators and gatekeepers of various kinds. Identify actual people when possible.

Kinds of things you'll need from the Community Arts Profile: information someone needs to learn about the community or genre for the activity to succeed. Note which information is already in the Community Arts Profile and that which still needs exploration. Many of these will be research activities in Step 4 that you haven't performed yet.

Resources needed: financial, technical, logistical, formal, and other requirements needed to make the activity happen.

Tasks: the jobs that someone needs to perform to carry out the activity. You may make these as detailed or broad as you like, depending on your context.

Big picture analysis: make three lists.

- CLAT steps included in the activity.
- CLAT steps done outside the activity, such as analysis of an event (Step 4) that someone else already did.
- Plans to address any missing steps in the future.

Figure 12. Things to Write Down When Designing a Sparking Activity

STEP 6

IMPROVE RESULTS

"Do not let any unwholesome talk come out of your mouths, but only what is helpful for building others up according to their needs, that it may benefit those who listen" (Eph 4:29).

Evaluate new works according to criteria agreed upon with the community. Remember that the goal of evaluating is construction, not destruction. The purpose of assessment is building up, not tearing down. Note, too, that a community can greatly reduce the need for critique by including the right people from the beginning of the co-creative process. People to include in the process are social and religious leaders, expert creators, and expert performers.

How do you decide what art is good or bad? Evaluation is complex. However, helpful assessment tools exist.

Trust the Local System

Groups usually share a sense of when an art work is good or not and have ways of communicating what needs to be fixed. Perform the research in "Aesthetics and Evaluation" (Step 4) to find out how correction normally works in the community. In some situations, they may get rid of inferior products by blocking them from future presentation and letting them die.

Evaluate According to Effects

In Step 3, you identified anticipated effects of new artistry. New works should influence a community's members to move toward kingdom goals. To evaluate whether a new work had the desired effect, observe and ask about people's responses to the new artistry. Did it have the effects you wanted? For example, an orator may intend to motivate people to join a parade celebrating their ethnic identity. However, if participants watch the speaker distractedly and then go home, the oration failed.

Relax, but Keep Learning

You can't study everything, so do this:

- Watch people's reactions.
- Listen to what they say.
- Regularly conduct research activities related to the genres you're working with (see Step 4 for examples)—maybe conduct one activity a week or month.
- Identify what kinds of evaluation should happen when.

Identify What Kinds of Evaluation Should Happen, and When

Evaluation can take place during the initial creation of a work. It can also happen after a composer has presented his or her work.

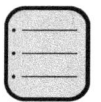 **Perform the activities described in Figure 13 below. (Some people call this "Critical Contextualization.") You will probably want to include evaluation at more than one point in the Creating Local Arts Together process.**

AN APPROACH TO EFFECTIVE EVALUATION

Identify and work through local social structures, and together define criteria for evaluating both existing and new works. Before bringing people together, identify the following aspects of the artistic event:

Elements: these should include how the work utilizes space, materials, participants, shape through time, performance features, feeling, content, themes, and community values.

Purpose(s): these could include to educate, motivate to action, and so on.

People: to include in the process of evaluation. These people need to have the knowledge, skills, and respect necessary to critique various elements. You may also want to include people from a variety of age and social groups.

Objects: that can provide a focal point and reference for discussion, so that you don't have to rely exclusively on memory for critique. These could include song texts, drama scripts, musical notation, masks, dance moves, and video and audio recordings.

Gather the people you identified. Show or demonstrate the art work, then follow these steps:

1. Together **affirm** the aspects of the creation that work well.
2. **Discuss** what meanings people received, how natural the work felt according to the genre, how well it represents their community, and if people think it will produce the purposes you decided on.
3. **Encourage** the creators to do something even better based on the evaluation.

Figure 13. An Approach to Effective Evaluation

STEP 7

CELEBRATE AND INTEGRATE FOR CONTINUITY

We don't just want to see new arts created for the kingdom once, but again and again and again. So it's also essential to plan for the future. A good place to start is to reflect with the community on the ways that they teach each other things like new songs, dances, and carving skills. If possible, their plans should include these means of transmission. To continue creating, a community's members may decide to repeat sparking activities like workshops or commissioning. Existing social groups like dance associations or literacy clubs may also have motivation to keep creating. Or communities might decide to form new groups that meet regularly to help members create for kingdom purposes.

If you have been following the CLAT process, there's not much more to say about integrating and celebrating. This is because the most important way to keep something good going is to start it in the right way. This process encourages you to make relationships, encourage others to create, get to know and value artists, plan, include all of the important artists and decision-makers in sparking activities, and help make artistic products and their presentation better.

To help you and your community keep thinking about making things last, we've included several bits of advice. As you reflect on these guidelines, you'll realize that they sometimes work counter to each other. Well, that's the way life is. If the community listens to God and grows in wisdom, they'll do fine.

Encourage the Community to Make Intentional Creativity a Habit

Go through the co-creative cycle in this manual again: Steps 1–7. The more the cycle is used by a community, the more it will become a familiar, regular process that flows naturally and efficiently through members' lives.

Encourage Continuity in Arts That Make the Most Unique Contributions to the Kingdom of Heaven

Globalization, urbanization, missionary activity, wars, and other factors often (though certainly not always) lead to the devaluation of and declining interest in the art forms of minority communities. The end of Revelation 21 suggests that elements of every culture will last into Heaven. When we all sing, dance, act, paint, and preach and teach in similar ways, we impoverish the global church on Earth and in Heaven (at least at the beginning). So don't assume that global trends are necessarily God's plans. Every bit of God-created diversity we can experience helps us know God better.

Encourage Continuity in Arts That Are Most Fragile

We should take special note of the artists and their art forms that are located in the world's margins. God's image is there.

Encourage Continuity in Arts That Are Most Likely to Flourish

We want new artistry to make positive differences in a community, so innovations that spread like wildfire can be and do great things.

Keep Praying and Helping to Fulfill Jesus's Prayer

Jesus taught us to pray and act upon these words: "Our Father in heaven, hallowed be your name, your kingdom come, your will be done, on earth as it is in heaven" (Matt. 6:9–10). Your community can continue to create in ways that will connect Heaven to Earth in ways beyond your imagination!

CLOSING 1

Community Arts Profile (CAP) Outline

We've created a file that provides spaces to describe and capture the results of activities related to the manual that you and a community do: http://ethnodoxologyhandbook.com/manual. Essentially, it restates many of the manual's sections so you know where to include results of activities you perform. You will replace the capitalized words with words appropriate to your context. For example, COMMUNITY NAME would be substituted with the name of the community you're working with, such as Sakha, the Bach clan, or l'Eglise Catholique de Tchinga. You are free to modify the structure, categories, and content of your CAP however you'd like. What follows is an example of the table of contents of a CAP yet to be filled in.

<COMMUNITY NAME>

Name of arts advocate(s):

Dates of work represented by this document:

SUMMARIZE PLANS, ACTIVITIES, RESULTS

- Creating Local Arts Together cycles completed (to any degree)
- List of events and genres researched (to any degree)

CREATING LOCAL ARTS TOGETHER CYCLE: <NUMBER>, FOR <KINGDOM GOAL(S)>

Step 1: Meet COMMUNITY and Its Artistic Genres
- Take a first glance at a community
- Take a first glance at a community's arts
- Take a first glance at a community's goals
- Start exploring a community's social and conceptual life
- Summarize results and challenges of this step

Step 2: Specify Kingdom Goals
- Help a community discover its kingdom goals
- Describe the one or two goals to focus on now
- Summarize results and challenges of this step

Step 3: Connect Genres to Goals
- Describe the process of the discussion of effects, content, genre, and events
- List the effects, content, genre, and event chosen
- Summarize results and challenges of this step

Step 4: Analyze Genres and Events
- Decide what research you will perform
- Perform research, entering results in "Descriptions of Artistic Genres"
- Summarize results and challenges of this step

Step 5: Spark Creativity
- Describe familiar methods of composition
- Identify opportunities to exploit and barriers to overcome
- Decide on the type of activity
- Design a new activity or modify an existing one that helps communities reach their goals
- Perform the activity
- Summarize results and challenges of this step

Step 6: Improve Results
- Choose and modify an approach to evaluation and improvement
- Perform the approach to evaluation and improvement
- Summarize results and challenges of this step

Step 7: Celebrate and Integrate for Continuity
- Choose what to integrate and celebrate
- Plan actions to keep good things going
- Summarize results and challenges of this step

DESCRIPTIONS OF ARTISTIC GENRES: <GENRE NAME>

A. Event Analysis: EVENT NAME
- Brief description
- First glance at the event
- Performance lenses on an event

B. Artistic Aspects of an Event
- Music
- Drama
- Dance
- Oral verbal arts
- Visual arts
- Interrelationships between formal elements of the event

C. Broader Cultural Context of an Event
- Artists
- Creativity
- Language
- Transmission and change
- Cultural dynamism
- Identity and power
- Aesthetics
- Time
- Emotions
- Subject matter
- Community values shown
- Communal investment

D. Explore How a Christian Community Relates Artistically to Its Broader Church and Cultural Context: CHURCH NAME
- Discover a Christian community's arts
- Compare a Christian community's use of arts with that of its surrounding communities
- Evaluate how arts currently fulfill a Christian community's purposes
- Apply tools available in the full Creating Local Arts Together manual, especially the heart arts questionnaire and the worship wheel
- Evaluate worship meetings using biblical principles
- Assess a multicultural Christian community's art
- Interpret Scripture well

CLOSING 2

Summary Decision Rubric

This format will help you succinctly describe a community's decisions from Steps 1, 2, and 3.

_____ will prepare
_{COMMUNITY}

_____ that includes enactment of
_{EVENT}

_____ with
_{GENRE(S)}

_____ to produce
_{CONTENT}

_____ that help
_{EFFECTS ON PEOPLE}

_____ move toward
_{COMMUNITY}

_____.
_{KINGDOM GOAL}

CLOSING

3

Creating Local Arts Together (CLAT) Summary

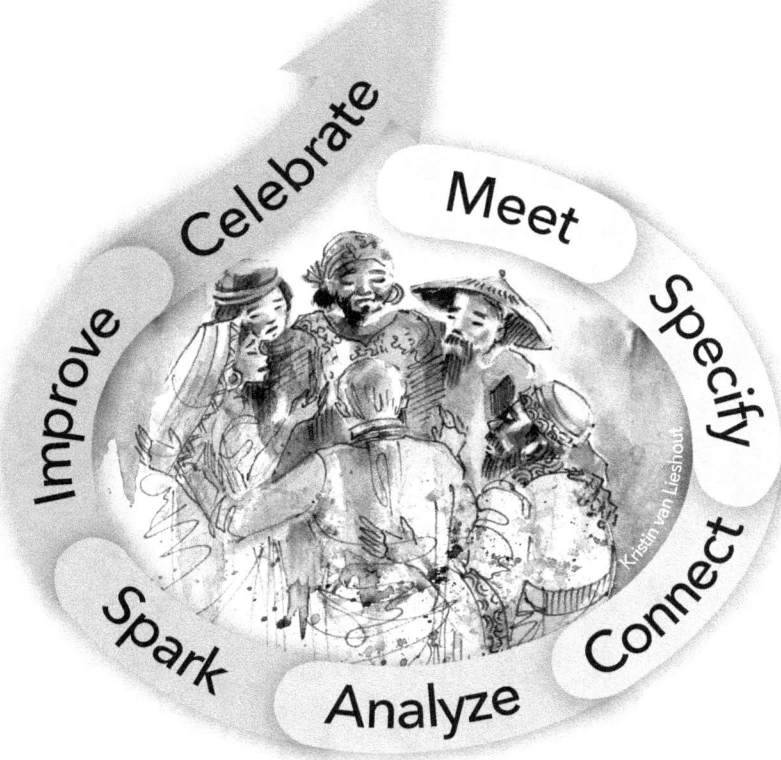

Meet a Community and Its Artistic Genres. Explore artistic and social resources that exist in the community.

Specify Kingdom Goals. Discover the kingdom goals that the community wants to work toward.

Connect Genres to Goals. Community chooses an artistic genre and activities that can help it meet its goals.

Analyze Genres and Events. Describe the event as a whole. Describe its artistic forms as arts. Describe the forms in relationship to broader cultural context. Detailed knowledge of the art forms is crucial to sparking (inspiring) creativity. It is important for improving what is produced, and it is necessary for integrating new works into the community.

Spark Creativity. Community implements activities to inspire creativity within the genres and events they have chosen.

Improve Results. Community evaluates results of the sparking activities and makes them better.

Celebrate and Integrate for Continuity. Plan and implement ways that this new kind of creativity can continue into the future. Identify more contexts where the new and old arts can be displayed and performed.

www.ingramcontent.com/pod-product-compliance
Lightning Source LLC
Chambersburg PA
CBHW051421070526
44584CB00023B/3522